DISCOVE

D0868193

BIRDS

AN INTRODUCTION TO THE BIRDS OF NIGERIA

ANNE NASON

Photographs by
IAN NASON

Sponsored by

Mobil

MOBIL PRODUCING NIGERIA UNLIMITED
(Operator of NNPC/Mobil Joint Venture)

for the
NIGERIAN CONSERVATION FOUNDATION

NCF

Pisces Publications
The Nature Conservation Bureau Limited

Published by Pisces Publications, 1992.

ISBN 1 874357 00 5

British Library Cataloguing-in-Publication Data.
A catalogue record for this book is available from the British Library.

Designed and produced by the Nature Conservation Bureau Limited, 36 Kingfisher Court, Hambridge Road, Newbury, Berkshire, UK.
Printed by Information Press, Oxford, UK.

This book is dedicated to our two grandsons who live in Kaduna.
I hope they will grow up to enjoy the beautiful birds of Nigeria
as much as we have.

LITTLE BEE-EATER

CONTENTS

ACKNOWLEDGEMENTS

Firstly, I would like to express my sincere thanks to 'Mobil Producing Nigeria' and its Managing Director, Mr Alfred Koch, for their generosity in funding this book on behalf of the Nigerian Conservation Foundation. The aim of the book is to inspire an interest in birds and their conservation in the young people of Nigeria. It is in their hands that the future of the country lies.

I am also most grateful to Tasso Leventis, Dr Pius Anadu, Philip Hall and Carolyn Knight of the NCF for their advice and encouragement throughout the writing of this book.

Many others have contributed their help and professional advice, and I would especially like to thank the following:
Professor John Elgood, formerly of the University of Ibadan.
Dr Mike Dyer, former Project Officer of the Hadejia Wetlands Project and previously of Ahmadu Bello University, Zaria.
Dr Nonie Coulthard and Ken Smith of the Royal Society for the Protection of Birds.
Dr Humphrey Crick of the British Trust for Ornithology for the use of seven photographs.
Mark Cocker, an independent Natural History consultant, for his editorial help.
Paul Goriup and Peter Creed of the Nature Conservation Bureau.

Finally, I owe a huge debt of gratitude to my husband Ian, whose photographs inspired the book in the first place. Together we visited most of the best bird-watching sites in the country, during the six years we lived in Nigeria.

Anne Nason

AUTHOR'S NOTE

As the common names of birds vary according to the different regions of Africa, I have followed the names used by Serle, Morel and Hartwig in their 'Field Guide to the Birds of West Africa' published by Collins. Some of the Latin names also vary according to different authorities, so again I have referred to the same source, as this is the Field Guide most often used by birdwatchers in Nigeria.

Many of the photographs were taken at the International Institute for Tropical Agriculture in Ibadan, so when referring to the Institute in the text I have used the abbreviation 'IITA', the name by which it is usually known.

In the chapters with photographs and descriptions of birds there are many common birds not included, but it is outside the scope of this book to cover all of them. I have simply chosen as broad a selection as possible.

Anne Nason

A FOREWORD
FROM THE PRESIDENT OF NCF,
CHIEF S.L. EDU, MFR

Nigeria's unique wildlife and countryside are disappearing rapidly under the relentless onslaught of a rapidly growing population. With over 100 million people, and an annual growth rate of 2.9 - 3.4%, the country's population will double within 20 years. Since more people means more demand for farmland, fuelwood, bushmeat, shelter and grazing land, this massive population increase will undoubtedly put intolerable pressure on the nation's remaining wilderness areas.

As an environmental watchdog, the NCF is naturally concerned about this imminent loss of our native flora and fauna which are not only a source of income for our rural population, but also provide recreation and inspiration for our urban dwellers. By protecting our forests, woodlands and wetlands, we preserve the full range of biological diversity available within our borders. This in turn leaves our options open for future developments in medicine, agriculture, animal husbandry, forestry and the chemical industry.

There is no knowing which plant (or animal) thought to be useless today will provide the cure for cancer, AIDS, leprosy or some other unknown disease. The rosy periwinkle, a plant that grows wild in the forests of Madagascar, and cultivated as an ornamental plant in Nigeria, is a fascinating example of how a 'useless' plant can become a money spinner. Two drugs, vincristine and vinblastine, derived from this plant are today used in the treatment of childhood leukaemia. It has also been reported that an extract from a plant found in the Korup forest, Western Cameroon, has tested positive to anti-cancer properties (BBC 24 January, 1990). This plant is so obscure, it doesn't even have a common name! Now, think of where mankind would be if these plants had been destroyed before their usefulness was discovered? To ensure that future generations of Nigerians continue to enjoy the benefits of our countryside and wildlife heritage, the NCF has embarked on a self-imposed mission of promoting the judicious use of our country's living resources.

INTRODUCTION

Nigeria has some of the most beautiful and interesting birds in the world. Because it is such a large country, stretching from the beaches and mangrove swamps of the Gulf of Guinea through the remnants of the rainforest to the savannas and thornscrub of the north, it provides a home, or 'habitat', for a fascinating variety of birds. All of these birds have become specially adapted to a particular environment, for example the huge numbers of water birds which live in the wetlands, or the birds which live in the depths of the rainforest. One of the enjoyments of studying birds is to learn some of the amazing secrets of nature which have taken scientists centuries to uncover. 'Ornithology' is the study of birds and future ornithologists still have years of exciting work ahead to reveal more of these fascinating facts. Over 850 species of birds have been recorded throughout the country, but species new to Nigeria are still being discovered, like the Bare-headed Rock-fowl which was found in the forests of a remote part of Cross River State in 1988. This curious looking bird which resembles a bald chicken, nests in caves deep in the forest, so had previously escaped detection by birdwatchers in this country.

WHY STUDY BIRDS?

Birds and other animals have always played an important part in African folktales, showing that in the past the peoples of Africa were keen observers of the natural world. These tales were often used to try and explain the habits of birds and animals, such as 'Why the Coucal is so feeble', or 'How the Leopard got his Spots'. For centuries, people in villages lived in reasonable harmony with nature, only clearing enough forest to grow their own food and trapping a few animals and birds to provide meat for their own use. However, with today's huge population explosion and the growth of large cities, many people are no longer in touch with nature and do not understand the relationship of human beings with other living things and their habitat, or to put it in scientific terms, the 'ecosystem'. Birds are an integral part of this ecosystem, so in order to know why we should study birds, we must first understand what the word means.

What is the Ecosystem?

All life on earth is dependent upon the sun. Plants grow by converting the sun's energy into food by the process of 'photosynthesis' and all insects, animals, birds and humans are either directly or indirectly dependent upon plants for their food. This is best illustrated by studying simple food chains and more complex food webs, where several food chains interact with each other.

Food Chains:

We ourselves feed directly on plants as fruit, vegetables, or grains like wheat, guinea corn, rice and millet or indirectly by eating meat from animals or poultry which have fed on plants. This is a simple food chain, which shows how interdependent all forms of life are upon another. Another example of a simple food chain is illustrated below:

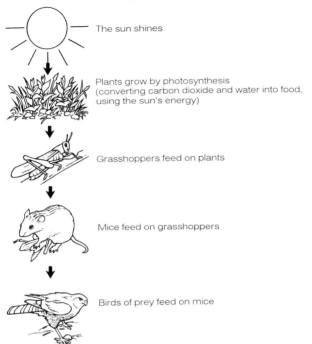

The sun shines

Plants grow by photosynthesis (converting carbon dioxide and water into food, using the sun's energy)

Grasshoppers feed on plants

Mice feed on grasshoppers

Birds of prey feed on mice

Now to see how this simple food chain interacts with other chains, we need to look at a food web:

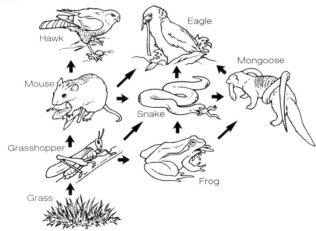

It is obvious therefore, that if any links of this chain are destroyed, every other link will be affected too.

Birds as an 'Early Warning System'

Studying birds can alert us to what is going wrong in our environment, as birds are excellent environmental indicators. This can be illustrated by looking at some of the problems which have occurred in the developed world. Some years ago in Europe it was discovered that the reason why birds of prey like the Peregrine were declining in numbers was that the shells of their eggs had become so unnaturally thin. The parent birds could not avoid breaking these during incubation, with the result that no chicks were hatching. Scientists found that the bodies of the adult Peregrines contained very high levels of the insecticide DDT and this was causing the egg-shells to be so fragile. The falcons were at the top of a similar food chain to the one illustrated above and had absorbed the DDT by eating small birds. These small birds had in turn fed on the grain sprayed with insecticide to kill the insect pests attacking the plants. If scientists had not been interested in the fate of Peregrines, we might never have known about the devastating effects of DDT, and that in the end would have seriously affected human beings. DDT has now been banned and today less harmful chemicals are being used. However, great care must still be taken, as scientists do not know all the long-term effects of such pesticides.

Another example shows how birds can be indicators of habitat quality. In recent years some rivers in Europe became so polluted with chemicals discharged from factories that the fish died and the type of birds called kingfishers, which lived on the fish, also disappeared as a result. When the pollution was controlled and the rivers became clean again, both the fish and the kingfishers returned. The presence of kingfishers on a river, therefore, is a symbol of a healthy river, which indicates where a human population can find clean drinking water.

Seabirds eat the same species of fish as we do, so any decline in their population can alert us to a pollution problem in the sea. Another problem they can indicate is over-fishing, which happened recently in the Shetland Islands to the north of Scotland. Fishermen were catching so many sand-eels that the seabirds could no longer catch enough to feed their young. Recently laws have been passed in Britain to stop over-fishing in this area, to allow time for the fish stocks to recover. In future the catch must be strictly controlled so that the fish can sustain their populations. Hopefully, in time, the seabirds will be able to breed again.

As we have just seen, the developed countries have made many mistakes in the past which they are now having to put right, so conservation (the protection of animals and their habitat) has become a very important issue. In developing countries like Nigeria it is vital to prevent people making the same mistakes, but already much of the rainforest has been cut down causing serious problems to the ecology of the southern part of the country. Once the rainforest is destroyed, the nutrients in the soil are quickly leached away by the heavy rainfall and eventually only infertile land is left. In the north, the over-grazing of live-stock has affected the environment, and parts of Borno State especially, are now suffering from 'desertification', (the land is becoming a desert). A good indicator of this is the fact that bird species which were once found only in the arid areas of Niger are now found in northern Nigeria. But not only are the birds affected; some villages north of Gashua are being smothered by sand dunes and the people are becoming refugees in their own country. Once again, studying birds has alerted us to the danger signals in the environment. Fortunately, conservation is beginning to become an important issue in Nigeria too, but every effort must be made to develop people's awareness to environmental problems.

Wherever you live in Nigeria, it is important to note the different types of birds which live in your area, to have an idea of their numbers, and whether they are common or uncommon. If you no longer see so many birds, some species disappear altogether, or new species arrive, ask yourself the question WHY? Perhaps there are too many trees being cut down in your neighbourhood, the rivers are becoming polluted, or the desert is encroaching? Remember, our own welfare is closely tied up with that of birds. If birds are affected, human beings will ultimately be affected too.

The Enjoyment of Birdwatching

Another reason for studying birds is that it can open your eyes to a whole new, interesting world which you may not know even exists. The beauty of many Nigerian birds is spectacular and many of the most colourful species are relatively easy to spot without having to go to special birdwatching areas. Even in Lagos compounds there are Senegal Kingfishers with their bright blue and grey plumage and striking red bills, noisy flocks of Senegal Wood-hoopoes searching for insects in the trees with their long, curved bills and iridescent sunbirds sipping nectar from the brightly coloured tropical flowers. Kestrels have colonised the tall office blocks of Lagos Island, nesting on ledges high above the crowded streets, whilst Black Kites soar high over the city in the dry season. Even Cattle Egrets 'have come to town' and stalk sedately round the Ikoyi golf course stabbing at insects in the grass and Shikras boldly take lizards from the walls of suburban houses.

Watching the way birds behave can be very revealing, and all you need is patience and sharp eyes. Many towns and villages throughout the country have colonies of Village Weavers, which in the breeding season chatter incessantly in their chosen nesting trees. It is fascinating to watch the male birds flying backwards and forwards with long green strips skilfully torn from a banana or palm leaf, to weave together to make their beautifully constructed hanging nests. When the work is finished, the handsome yellow and black male bird hangs upside down from the nest, fluttering his wings invitingly, seeking a female to choose his nest to lay her eggs in. Sometimes weavers select palm trees and the nests hang from palm fronds like fruits on a tree.

If you want to attract birds to your compound, one sure way is to put out water for them in a shallow earthenware dish and then watch them fly down to drink and bathe. Notice the different ways that birds drink, and see how they preen their feathers after bathing. Try and observe the 'pecking order', by seeing which birds are dominant and chase away the weaker birds, and which birds give way to them. Courtship behaviour, when the male bird tries to attract the female in the breeding season, makes another fascinating study. Watch how the male dove inflates his throat and coos invitingly to impress the female, or flies up into the air to descend rapidly with outstretched wings, opening his tail like a fan as he glides downwards.

Bird-song is another marvel of nature. Even tiny birds can produce intricate songs and calls, and it adds to the enjoyment of birdwatching if you can identify their calls without even seeing the bird, in the same way that you can identify a friend calling when he or she is out of sight. Birds have different calls for different situations; one call may be an alarm signal to warn of danger approaching, another may be to attract a mate or to advertise the territory where a pair are building a nest, in order to keep other birds away.

These are just some of the reasons for studying birds, and now we can begin to answer the question: WHY DO WE NEED BIRDS?

1. For Food: Chickens have been domesticated for at least 4,500 years and are descended from the wild Jungle Fowl of south-east Asia. Chickens, like geese, ducks and turkeys are an important source of food both for their meat and eggs. Wild birds and eggs are also an important food source but must be harvested in a sustainable way so that enough breeding stock is preserved for the future.

2. For Pest Control: Birds eat insects like grasshoppers and locusts which are agricultural pests. Birds of prey help to control populations of harmful rodents whilst vultures act as natural rubbish disposers by cleaning up the carcases of dead animals and human refuse.

3. As Pollinators of Flowers: Birds like sunbirds help to pollinate flowers as they pass from one to another seeking nectar, in the same way as bees carry out pollination.

4. As Seed Dispersers: Birds carry fruit away from plants and disperse the seeds widely so that new plants have space to grow.

5. As Messengers: Homing pigeons were used to carry messages, (in a little container tied to their legs) before the advent of telephones and radios. Now they are used mainly as racing birds, for sport.

6. As Food Catchers: (Birds of prey like falcons and goshawks have been used for centuries, especially in the Middle East, to catch small animals and birds for their master's table, but Falconry is now mainly a sport). In parts of China, tame cormorants are used to catch fish. A ring is placed round the neck of the cormorant to prevent it swallowing the fish, and it is trained to bring the catch to the fishermen where it is rewarded with food.

7. To Protect Planes From Bird Strikes: Falcons are kept at some airports to keep flocks of birds away from the runways to prevent them being sucked into the jet engines of planes and causing a crash.

8. As Honey Guides: There are several species of birds called Honey-guides in Africa, because they guide hunters to wild bees' nests by fluttering in front of them and leading them to the nest. The bird's reward is to eat the grubs and the discarded pieces of honeycomb left behind by the hunter.

9. As a Source of Fertiliser: The droppings of seabirds are rich in phosphates. 'Guano', as the accumulated droppings are called, is an important source of fertiliser for farmers.

10. For Pleasure: The beauty of birds and their songs give pleasure to people.

11. For Art and Culture: Birds have featured strongly in art and religion in most cultures of the world. The Sacred Ibis is so called because it was revered by the Egyptians in the days of the Pharaohs. The beauty of birds and their song has often been extolled in verse, such as in the work of the English poet, John Keats' 'Ode to a Nightingale'. Birds like the eagle have become the symbol of strength and power, and are used in many coats of arms like that of Nigeria itself, while owls have become the symbol of wisdom and learning. Birds also feature in many African folktales, see Chapter Eleven.

12. For Their Feathers: In Africa feathers are mostly used for decoration, as in head-dresses and fans, but in cold countries feathers are used for their insulating properties in pillows, cushions and duvets.

13. As Warning Lights: Last, but by no means least, birds are vitally important indicators of the environment in this age when conservation has become a matter of life or death to the peoples of the world.

However, the problem of birds as pests themselves, must also be considered. This occurs when one species of bird increases enormously, usually as a result of changes being made to the environment which are particularly favourable to that species, and so upsetting the balance of nature. This has happened to some extent in the grain growing areas of northern Nigeria where the large numbers of Quelea birds have become a pest to farmers. In the past the Queleas were restricted by the amount of grass seed available but with more and more cereal crops being cultivated, the population of Queleas has exploded in response to this 'bonanza' of food. Birds of prey, which previously kept the population under control, can no longer kill enough to keep their numbers at a reasonable level.

The answer to this problem is to understand the birds and their habits in order to control them by biological means if possible, so that man and bird can achieve a reasonable balance. Research is currently being undertaken at the University of Maiduguri into ways of combating bird pests.

Chapter One

FACTS ABOUT BIRDS - THEIR EVOLUTION AND BIOLOGY

ORIGIN AND EVOLUTION

Birds probably evolved from small, light-boned, warm-blooded reptiles that ran on their hind legs. The first true bird appeared about 100 million years ago in the Cretaceous geological age, and birds still have some of the characteristics of their reptilian ancestors, like scales on their legs and the way they reproduce their young by laying eggs. The 'Archaeopteryx' is a famous fossil found in Bavaria in Germany, which shows features of both birds and reptiles, and has been dated at about 130 million years old. Over the millions of years since then, birds have evolved into many different forms, from the huge Ostrich to the tiny sunbird, and because they are warm-blooded, they have been able to adapt themselves to living in climates varying from the ice and snow of the Antarctic to the fringes of the hottest deserts. Throughout the world there are over 9,000 species of birds, of which Nigeria has approximately 840. Today birds are one of the most successful of all animal groups and are remarkably versatile. Although they are specialised for flight they can, with varying degrees of skill, walk, run, perch, climb, swim and dive as well.

The Structure of a Bird

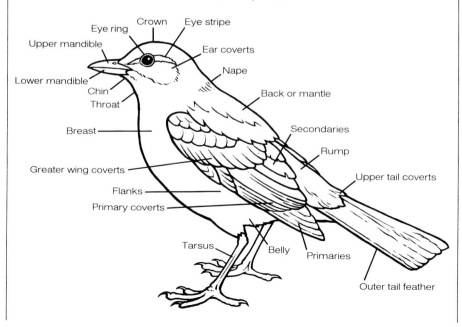

Flight

Birds are highly specialised flying machines. Their ability to fly allows them to range widely in search of food and to escape predators easily. In order to fly birds need to be very light, so they have hollow bones with air inside. Since evolving from reptiles, birds have lost heavy structures such as teeth and instead have a gizzard to grind up their food. This is a specially adapted part of the digestive system where the 'stomach' has developed thick, muscular walls. Birds need to swallow grit to help the grinding process as their food passes through it. They have no bladders so do not carry around extra water. The white part of their droppings is the equivalent of urine, and many species of birds eject pellets from their stomachs through their mouths so that indigestible bits of food are not carried round unnecessarily. Not all birds can fly, however; birds like the Ostrich of Africa and the Emu of Australia are too heavy to fly but can run very fast instead to enable them to escape from enemies.

Flying needs a great deal of energy, so birds have a large heart to pump oxygen into their blood. Air passes twice through the lungs with every breath in and out so that all the available oxygen can be used. Their body temperature is several degrees higher than a human's, and feathers provide excellent insulation to keep in their body heat. Birds have to overcome the pull of gravity in order to haul themselves into the air from the ground, and this is helped by the massive bundle of muscles which stretches from the wing-joint down to the deep keel on the breastbone.

The principle of flight is the same for both aircraft and birds, and it was by observing birds that man eventually invented the aeroplane. Wings are thicker at the front, tapering smoothly to a point at the back with the upper surface more curved and the lower surface flatter - an aerofoil shape just like the wing of a plane. When a bird beats its wings, the air moves farther and faster over the bulging upper surface than it does along the flat underside. This lowers the pressure of air above the wing and so the wing is lifted by the comparatively high pressure underneath.

The wing shape varies according to the lifestyle of the bird. The Swift's narrow scythe-shaped wings gives it great speed and endurance and it even sleeps on the wing, only coming to earth to nest. Vultures can soar for hours by spreading their huge broad wings to catch the updraughts of thermal air currents generated when the earth below them heats up. The broad, well-separated flight feathers of the wing-tips help to keep the birds airborne for hours. The tail feathers can be fanned out to use as brakes to slow down a landing. If you watch a Kestrel or Black-shouldered Kite hovering in the air, scanning the ground for its prey, you will see how the tail feathers are spread out and the wings tilt to maintain its balance while it literally 'hangs' in the sky. Birds like bulbuls and other forest birds which live in thick bush, need short, rounded wings for manoeuvrability.

In summary, the different types of wing shapes are:
1. Long and narrow for speed e.g. swifts and falcons.
2. Broad and long for soaring e.g. hawks and eagles.
3. Short and rounded for manoeuvrability e.g. forest birds.

Feathers

Adult birds are covered with large 'contour' feathers which provide smooth body contours to lessen the air resistance in flight as well as excellent insulation to keep the body warm. They also provide protection from injury. The soft feathers underneath the contour feathers, called down, are entirely for insulation. Feathers must function efficiently for a bird to fly, so they have to take great care of them. Preening, dust-bathing and water bathing are all essential activities to keep the feathers in prime condition. Birds have an oil-gland near the base of their tails which they use to keep their feathers waterproofed, and a preening bird will smear oil on its beak and then run its beak over its feathers to distribute the oil evenly. They rid themselves of parasites by dust-bathing, and it is a familiar sight to see domestic chickens doing this by sitting in a dusty place in the compound, fluffing out their feathers to powder them with dust. Birds frequently take water baths before a preening session and sunbathe too, by spreading out their wing feathers towards the sun. Cormorants always need to dry off their feathers after a fishing session, and they do this by sitting on a log or branch with outspread wings, which is a characteristic pose. Some birds even indulge in a curious practice called 'anting' by picking up ants in their bills and preening with them. It is thought that the formic acid excreted by the ant will rid them of parasites. As feathers receive a lot of wear and tear, they are moulted after the breeding season and replaced by new ones to keep the bird in perfect flying condition.

Although feathers are unique to birds, they are made of the same material that is found in hair, claws and hooves, a substance called keratin. The central portion of a feather, the quill, is rooted in the skin of the bird with muscles attached, so that the feathers are freely movable. On either side of the quill is the part of the feather called the vane. Each vane is made up of structures called barbs which link together with tiny hooks. This allows the bird to clean between and under the feathers and yet allows each feather to be 'zipped up' to provide a smooth, flat, waterproof surface. When a bird preens itself it makes sure all these hooks are linked together so the feathers are perfectly arranged for flying.

If you find a discarded feather on the ground, unhook the vane carefully in one or two places and then try closing it again by running it firmly through your fingers. You will then understand what a bird is doing when it preens its feathers - relinking the barbs which have become disturbed during flight. The down feathers have no

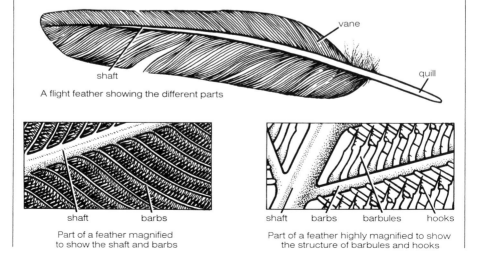

A flight feather showing the different parts

shaft   barbs
Part of a feather magnified
to show the shaft and barbs

shaft   barbs   barbules   hooks
Part of a feather highly magnified to show
the structure of barbules and hooks

hooks on the barbs, but fluff up to trap a layer of air next to the skin. When a bird is cold, it will fluff up its outer feathers too, making it look twice the size, in order to increase the insulating effect. Owls, which chiefly hunt by night, have special soft fringes along the edge of their flight feathers to muffle the sound of their approach, so they can pounce on their prey without warning.

We have already seen that feathers are essential for flight and are excellent insulators, but they have other uses as well. They provide perfect camouflage for ground-living birds like the Senegal Thick-knee, or the Bushfowl, both of which have dull brown, mottled plumage. Many female birds are duller than the males to conceal them from predators when they are on the nest. Male birds however, are often brightly coloured in order to attract a mate, and Africa has some of the world's most colourful birds, many of which are clothed in brilliant reds, blues, yellows and greens. Yet another use is demonstrated by the sandgrouse, which nests in the desert and has to fly some distance to find water. It soaks its breast feathers and then carries water to its thirsty chicks trapped in the down for them to suck the water from.

THE SENSES

Sight: Birds have exceptionally good eyesight and have huge eyes in comparison with their size. The Ostrich has the largest eye of any land animal, even larger than an elephant's and it is perfect for spotting danger in the open grasslands where they live. Birds see in colour, otherwise there would be no need for them to have bright plumage to attract a mate.

Sight is the dominant sense and birds of prey have eyesight many times sharper than our own. Their eyes are set right at the front of their head to give them stereoscopic (three dimensional) vision which is essential for judging distances accurately when diving on their prey. The Lizard Buzzard, for example, sits quietly on a branch, watching for movement below, and needs great speed and accuracy to catch a fast moving skink or agama lizard. Vultures, which feed on carrion, can spot a dead or dying animal from a great height. When one vulture is seen descending, other vultures from miles around follow it to investigate a likely source of food.

Owls are nocturnal, (which means that they are mainly active by night), so they have developed huge eyes which see in dim light. No bird however, can see in total darkness, so owls have very acute hearing as well. An owl cannot move its eyes in its sockets, but has an extremely flexible neck and can turn its head through almost a full circle in order to see behind it.

Apart from birds of prey, most other species of birds have eyes on the sides of their heads. This gives them a much wider field of vision but it means that they only have two dimensional sight. To compensate for this, a bird will cock its head from side to side to build up a three dimensional picture. If you see a West African Thrush on the ground, cocking its head as if it is listening carefully, it is really trying to judge the distance to its prey (often an earthworm) more accurately.

Birds have an upper and lower eyelid just as we do, which they only close when they sleep, but only owls, like humans, can blink their eyes. However, birds also have a third, semi-transparent eyelid, the nictitating membrane, which they can pull over their eyes for protection from glare in bright sunlight, (as we would wear dark glasses), or from dust or rain when they are flying. Birds often draw their nictitating membrane across their eyes when feeding young, as it affords some protection against the eagerly grabbing beaks of the hungry nestlings.

Hearing: A bird's hearing is also good - a vital necessity if it is to escape predators. Birds' ears are not normally visible, but are set just behind their eyes and covered with feathers. As we have mentioned, owls have particularly acute hearing in order to hear the squeaks of their prey in the dark. They mostly feed on small rodents like mice, and have one ear set slightly higher than the other to help them locate the sound with greater accuracy. The flattened disc of feathers that surround their eyes are thought to act as sound reflectors, in the same way that a satellite dish does.

Taste, Smell and Touch: These senses are less important to birds, and most birds probably have little sense of taste or smell, unlike most mammals to whom a sense of smell is essential in tracking prey in thick grass or dense undergrowth. However, this may be far too sweeping a statement and evidence is emerging that certain groups of birds may have a much more developed sense of smell than naturalists originally thought. There is much work to be done on this subject, but experiments on Turkey Vultures in North America have shown that these birds do much of their hunting by smell, so perhaps this is also true of African vultures.

The sense of taste is a particularly difficult sense to investigate, even in humans, but as birds have very few taste buds in comparison with mammals, it is thought that this sense is not well developed.

Some wading birds, like Whimbrels, have sensitive bills to probe the mud and pick up the vibrations of worms which are their main food.

BIRD PELLETS

Many birds produce pellets containing the undigested remains of their food, by regurgitating them through their beaks. In birds of prey the pellets are oval-shaped objects, formed of compressed fur or feathers and containing small bones and parts of large insects. Pellets are valuable to naturalists because they give evidence of the bird's diet and can be dissected to discover exactly what the bird has been feeding on.

Probably the easiest pellets to find are owl pellets, as owls often roost in the same tree during the day. Pellets can be picked up from the ground underneath, although care must be taken never to disturb a breeding owl.

How are they produced?

An owl will often swallow its prey whole, but if it is too large, it can be pulled apart first with the strong, hooked beak.

Once the food is swallowed, it passes down to the stomach where the soft parts are rapidly digested in the gizzard. The parts of the prey which cannot be digested however, like the bones, fur or feathers, are then squeezed into a compact mass in the gizzard. The pellet is finally coughed up or regurgitated through the beak. Because it has not passed through the intestine of the owl, it is therefore quite different from droppings. The pellets do not smell so are not unpleasant to work with.

Owls seem to produce two, or sometimes three, pellets each 24 hours. It probably takes about 6 to 8 hours between prey being eaten and any undigested remains being ejected from the mouth as a pellet.

The value of owl pellet studies

The solid remains contained in owl pellets can easily be extracted. They can often be identified, sometimes very precisely, as the bones are so little affected by digestion. Some of these bones are particularly valuable in identifying the prey of the owl. Small mammals, like mice or rats can be readily identified from their skulls and jawbones.

With a bit of detective work we can get a great deal of information about the owl:
1. We can identify precisely what it has been feeding on.
2. We can make deductions about the owl's hunting habits from the prey it has taken.
3. We can estimate the numbers of different kinds of prey it takes.
4. If we find out more about the prey animals themselves, we learn a great deal about food chains and the exact part the owl plays in them.

Owl pellets are composed of animal bones bound together with fur

HOW BIRDS HAVE ADAPTED TO THEIR HABITAT

The 'habitat' of a bird or animal simply means 'the place where it lives'. Over millions of years birds have diversified into more than 9,000 different species, all adapted to the variations in the habitats of the world. Within each type of habitat, every individual bird species follows a lifestyle that is slightly different from all its neighbours. This is called its 'ecological niche' and it enables many birds to live side by side without conflict. If two species ate exactly the same sort of food, one of them would probably become dominant and might eventually force its competitor to become extinct. However, because birds have adapted to such a wide variety of foods, many different species can live together in harmony. The swallows and swifts hawking for insects in the air do not compete with the leaf-warblers searching for ants and caterpillars amongst the leaves nor thrushes seeking for worms in the ground. The doves picking up seeds on the ground or eating berries in the trees are not in competition with sunbirds drinking nectar from the flowers, so they can all live together in the same habitat, occupying their own particular niches.

Beaks and Feet for Specialised Tasks

Birds have evolved different types of beaks and feet in order to cope with the varying ways in which they obtain their food. By looking at a bird it is often possible to guess what type of food it is likely to eat. However, it must be noted that although some birds rely upon one source of food only, others have a more varied diet. Seed eaters, for example, often feed insects to their nestlings in the breeding season. Some birds too, are opportunists and will eat other forms of food if they are readily available.

The best way of understanding these particular adaptations is to look at the type of food birds eat and then see what tools they need for the task:

1. Flesh-eating birds

Birds of prey need powerful talons (claws) with which to seize and kill their prey, and strong, hooked beaks to tear off strips of meat before swallowing it. The upper part of the beak is hooked at the tip and overlaps the lower mandible so a firm grip can be obtained to tear the meat from the bone. Large eagles like the Crowned Eagle and Martial Eagle can tackle animals as big as monkeys and have immensely strong talons and beaks. The prey is firmly grasped in their sharp talons and carried away to a place of safety to be devoured. The claws are sometimes used to kill the animal by piercing it in a weak spot.

Vultures, which live on carrion, need powerful beaks for tearing through the hide of a dead animal to get at the meat. Their heads and necks are mostly free of feathers, like the Hooded Vulture, so they can thrust them inside a carcass without getting their feathers matted with blood. As they do not kill their own prey, vultures do not have such powerful feet as eagles.

Smaller birds of prey such as the aptly named Lizard Buzzard, eat lizards or small birds and, not surprisingly, the Grasshopper Buzzard feeds mainly on grasshoppers and locusts. The feet of raptors (diurnal birds of prey) are usually bare and scaly, as tearing meat can be a messy business, and featherless feet are easier to keep clean. Snake-eating eagles like the Short-toed Eagle have tough scales on their legs to protect them from snake-bites and shorter toes to give them a better grip on a writhing snake. Most snake-eaters will cut off the snake's head first before swallowing the rest of the reptile whole.

Owls swallow their prey whole instead of tearing it, so their beaks are smaller, and their feet feathered to deaden the noise of their flight as they pounce on their unsuspecting prey. Their talons are extremely powerful and sharp, as like most birds of prey they seize their prey with their feet. Owls, though, usually transfer the victim to their beaks to carry it to a perch for swallowing, or feeding to their young.

Harrier Hawks have developed strange double-jointed legs for reaching into tree holes in search of bats, lizards and young birds, and it is a fascinating sight to watch such a large bird clinging to a tree trunk, flapping to retain its balance, while it investigates a likely hole. The yellow patch of skin around its eye flushes red at the prospect of enjoying a meal.

IMMATURE MARTIAL EAGLE

HARRIER HAWK

GREY HERON

2. Fish-eating birds

Herons, storks and egrets, which live mainly on fish and frogs, need long pincer-like bills to seize a fish swimming below the surface. The bird then turns the fish to swallow it head first. Their long legs allow them to wade deep into the water without wetting their feathers.

Kingfishers, like the Pied Kingfisher, catch fish in their massive bills by diving from a perch, or hovering above the water, so long legs would be a hindrance. The kingfisher will first break the bones of a larger fish by battering it against its perch to make it easier to swallow. The fish is always swallowed head first in order to prevent the fins catching in the bird's throat.

Birds of prey like Ospreys and Fish-Eagles catch fish just below the surface of the water by swooping down and grasping them with both feet at once. Sometimes the Osprey goes underwater in its efforts to hold onto the fish, but it can close its nostrils as it submerges. The fish is held in its powerful talons as it flies to a perch in a tall tree to consume it, and rough scales on the soles of its feet give it a better grip on the struggling fish. Fishing owls have no feathers on their feet and legs as fish scales are very difficult to remove from fluffy feathers.

Swimming and diving birds, like shags and cormorants, which catch fish by chasing them underwater, also have hooks on the tips of their upper mandibles to hold the slippery fish. All swimming birds' feet have webs or flaps of skin stretched between the toes, which greatly enhance their swimming ability. Their legs are set well back to give the maximum thrust through water, which is why swimming birds like ducks walk with such an ungainly waddle on land.

The pelican's huge pouched bill is used to scoop up fish while the bird is swimming. These birds often move in small groups and fish in unison, all scooping with their bills at the same time.

BLACK-WINGED STILT

3. Shore-feeders

This category includes the many waders, or long-legged birds that feed on the small crustaceans, shellfish and worms which live in the mud of lake and seashores. It includes birds like the Whimbrel, Black-winged Stilt, and Bar-tailed Godwit which have developed long legs to keep their feathers from becoming water-logged as they wade in the shallow water, and long bills to probe the mud for food. All these birds, which are migrants to Nigeria during the dry season, feed on mudflats, rice paddies and along the shores of estuaries and lagoons but each has a slightly different shaped bill for its specific method of feeding. The Whimbrel has a long decurved bill for probing the mud, whilst the Bar-tailed Godwit's is slightly upturned at the end and feeds by probing deeply or moving its bill from side to side in the shallow water. The stilt has extremely long pink legs so it can wade into deeper water, and a fine straight bill with which it searches the water for food with jabbing and sweeping movements.

4. Insect-eating birds

Many birds are insectivorous but here too, there is an infinite variety of methods for obtaining their insect prey. Birds which forage in the leaves for ants and other small insects, like the leaf warblers and the tiny Yellow White-eye, need slender pointed bills. Bee-eaters, which hawk insects from a perch, have long curved bills to allow them to catch bees in flight without being stung, but before swallowing a bee the bird will dash it against a branch to remove the sting. The long, red, curved bill of the Senegal Wood-hoopoe is used for probing the bark of trees for insects hidden in crevices.

The pointed bill of the woodpecker is ideal for boring holes in decaying trees either to obtain grubs, or to use as a nesting hole. Woodpeckers use their long sticky tongues to extract the grubs. They have two toes pointing forwards and two backwards so that they can cling more easily to the trunk as they climb upwards, and strong, stiff tail feathers to help support them. To observe a woodpecker feeding, watch it from a concealed position if possible because if it sees someone watching, it will invariably go round to the other side of the trunk to keep out of sight. However, woodpeckers often give away their presence by the sound of their loud 'drumming', made by tapping their beaks rapidly against the trunk of a tree. Their necks are specially strengthened to withstand the stress of this 'hammering'.

Swifts are the most aerial of all birds, and feed by hawking for flying insects high in the sky. Their beak opens very widely to allow them to scoop up flying insects, and the bristles round their bill are probably helpful in trapping them. As swifts feed, drink and sleep in flight and only land to enter a nest-hole, their legs are extremely short and their four tiny claws all point forwards to help them to hang on to vertical surfaces. Swallows and martins also feed by catching flying insects but they usually hunt at lower levels, particularly over water, so competition with swifts is reduced. Keen eyesight is needed by all these insect 'hunters', to spot their prey whilst flying at high speed.

Flycatchers also catch insects in the air, but birds like the Spotted Flycatcher which is a dry-season migrant to Nigeria, fly from a perch to seize a passing insect, often returning to the same perch to eat it.

Nightjars have exploited yet another 'niche' by feeding at night on the abundant supply of moths. They have huge eyes to see in dim light and enormously wide mouths fringed with long bristles. Their feathers are well camouflaged with a 'cryptic' pattern to keep them hidden by day. At night they can sometimes be seen in the headlights of a car on laterite roads as they fly up in front of an advancing vehicle.

5. Seed-eating birds

Seeds provide a rich source of food for many species. Birds which feed mainly on seeds have short, stout bills so they can crush the seed and remove the husk before eating it. Common finches like Senegal Fire-finches, Bronze Mannikins and Red-cheeked Cordon-bleus are relatively tame so their method of dealing with seeds can easily be observed. They hold the seed in their stocky beaks, crush it, then reject the husk with their tongues before eating the kernel. They spend much of their time hopping on the ground, foraging for seeds. Birds like the Red and Fire-crowned Bishops of the savanna, cling to the millet or guinea corn stems to eat the seeds from the ripening plant.

6. Fruit-eating birds

Fruit is another important source of food and fruit-eating, or frugivorous, birds have evolved different types of beaks to exploit them. Parrots have deep hooked bills to tear open the skin of the fruit. Grey Parrots which are found in the forest zone, chiefly feed on the outer flesh of the oil palm nut. Like all parrots, their feet are specially adapted for climbing and clinging to branches to reach the fruit. They will also use their feet to pick up a piece of fruit to pass it to their beaks in the same way that we would use our hands. These beautiful parrots are a declining species in Nigeria because of the large numbers being taken from their nests to be sold as cage birds, often when they are too young to survive. In the wild it is a wonderful sight to see them flying fast and

VIEILLOT'S BARBET

free above the forest, calling loudly as they fly, but all too often they are confined to tiny cages to spend their lives in captivity.

The large bills of the forest Hornbills are also adapted for fruit-eating, but these massive bills, which in the male birds are even larger with their huge horny casques, are much lighter than they look, and are ideal for reaching fruit and berries on outlying branches in tall forest trees. Barbets like the comic looking Bearded Barbet of the savanna area and the Tooth-billed Barbet of the forest zone, are also mainly fruit-eating and have large chunky bills with 'toothed' edges which help to crush the shiny-skinned fruits they feed on.

6. Nectar-eaters

In Nigeria the sunbirds occupy roughly the same ecological niche as the hummingbirds of the Americas. Their long decurved bills are specifically designed for probing the slender flower-tubes of tropical plants for nectar, or picking small insects from the surrounding foliage. The tiny Yellow-bellied Sunbird with its metallic green and purple plumage, is the commonest sunbird of Lagos compounds where it can be observed flitting from flower to flower, constantly on the move in its endless search for food. The larger Scarlet-breasted Sunbird, which has a particularly long, curved bill is the commonest sunbird in savanna areas like Kaduna, where it is frequently seen in compounds wherever there are trees in blossom. It is easier to observe as it is relatively unafraid of the presence of humans.

Chapter Two

BIRD BEHAVIOUR

PART ONE: BREEDING BEHAVIOUR

Courtship

The behaviour of animals is one of the most exciting aspects of natural history as it is full of action and drama. It is during the breeding season that birds are most active and therefore easier and more interesting to observe. Not only are many dressed in the bright colours of their breeding plumage, but they perform elaborate courtship rituals, defend territories aggressively, sing or call loudly, build complicated nests and industriously feed their young. A great deal of the information we have on the breeding behaviour of birds is due to patient observation by ornithologists in the field. In the last few years, with the invention of new scientific techniques, scientists have been able to unravel even more fascinating secrets by using fibre-optic probes to see into nesting burrows without disturbing the occupants, or by watching the courtship of nocturnal birds with image-intensifying equipment which can 'see' in the dark. However, there is plenty for the ordinary observer to watch with no other equipment than a good pair of eyes, or if possible, a pair of binoculars.

In Nigeria, some birds breed in the dry season and others in the wet season, so breeding behaviour can be observed, in different species, all the year round. However, dry season Palearctic migrants do not breed in Nigeria at all but leave this country during the rains to go to Europe to nest, as we will see in part two of this chapter. Other species breed elsewhere in Africa, like the White-throated Bee-eater which moves north to breed on the borders of Nigeria and Niger at the start of the rains.

Breeding Plumage

Just as human beings dress up in their best clothes for a marriage ceremony, so birds put on their brightest plumage in the breeding season. In some species, like the Red Bishop, for example, or the Pin-tailed Whydah, the males acquire a completely different plumage. In the dry season both these birds are indistinguishable from their females with their brownish, nondescript feathers, but with the arrival of the rains they start to develop their very distinctive breeding plumage. The Red Bishop of the Guinea savanna zone is conspicuously dressed in black and red and can sometimes be seen at the edges of cornfields, especially where there is water, zooming along in a jerky display flight like a toy helicopter. The Pin-tailed Whydah changes into a smart black and white bird with a red bill and an enormously long ribbon-like tail. In flight he proceeds with undulating bounds, and it is surprising he manages to remain airborne at all with such a disproportionately long tail.

The male Broad-tailed Paradise Whydah, which is more common in the extreme

BROAD-TAILED PARADISE WHYDAH

COMMON GARDEN BULBUL

north of Nigeria, has a broader tail and an even more comic appearance. The cock-bird likes to sit on the topmost branch of a bush, displaying his splendid tail to the best advantage. Males with the longest and most spectacular tails are likely to attract a mate most easily. After the breeding season is over, the feathers drop out, or moult, to be replaced by the less conspicuous dry season plumage. This ability to moult their feathers also means that if feathers are lost or damaged the bird can grow new ones to keep them in perfect flying condition.

In species where the male and female have a different appearance (sexual dimorphism is the scientific term) it is usually the male bird which has the brighter plumage. The female with her dull colouring will be less conspicuous while incubating the eggs on the nest, although in some cases, like the Paradise Flycatcher, the brightly coloured male also incubates the eggs. The Painted Snipe is one bird where the normal roles are reversed and the female has the more distinctive plumage. Although, of course, she lays the eggs, it is the duller-looking male who incubates them and looks after the young. Once again, nature springs surprises! In many species, like the Common Garden Bulbul and the Splendid Glossy Starling, the male and female are identical, while in others the differences are only slight. By contrast, in some birds of prey, such as the Kestrel, the female is not only larger than the male, but a different coloration as well, which makes the identification of raptors particularly difficult.

Courtship Rituals

In order to attract a mate, birds 'display' to their partner before mating takes place. All birds have some form of courtship display but the bird that has the most vigorous and attractive display, is likely to be the most dominant and fittest individual of that species, so has the best chance of a successful mating. Thus display is a factor in natural selection, the survival of the fittest, which is one of the key principles of evolution. Observing this behaviour and contrasting the courtship rituals of different species can make a fascinating study, but remember that birds are particularly wary in the breeding season and may not behave naturally if they know they are being watched.

One of the most spectacular displays is practised by the beautiful azure-blue Abyssinian Roller which tumbles and 'rolls' in flight with amazing aeronautical skill, while at the same time uttering a succession of harsh cries. The long tail streamers probably help to increase the bird's manoeuvrability as well as enhancing his handsome appearance.

Birds of prey also have spectacular courtship display flights. The males may swoop up and down in the air, closing their wings and diving hundreds of metres, then sweeping upwards again with flapping wings. Sometimes both partners may wheel and dive together with the female turning over on her back, locking claws with her mate and tumbling through the air, like the magnificent African Fish Eagle. The Harrier Hawk displays by flying in a succession of short ascents followed by short, steep dives. All these aerial acrobatics provide a thrilling spectacle for the birdwatcher.

Some male birds will even pass food to their mates in flight, which calls for precision flying, as the male drops the prey and the female rolls over on her back in mid-air to catch it. This courtship feeding (in which the male brings food to the female) has two purposes. Firstly it strengthens the 'pair-bond' between the two birds and secondly the extra food helps with the female's egg-production. Male cuckoos will bring caterpillars to feed the female, who behaves like a young bird, or fledgling, fluttering her wings and begging for food. Male Pied Kingfishers will offer fish to a prospective mate, and in most species of bee-eater the male presents insects to his partner prior to mating.

Storks practise bill-clattering and neck-bending and Crowned Cranes have evolved an elaborate 'dance' in their courtship rituals. Grey Hornbills 'bray' loudly from the tops of trees, and owls, who do their courting at night when extravagant displays would be wasted, have a whole range of calls, grunts and bill-clickings. Some birds, like the Spur-winged Plover, become very aggressive in the breeding season and will circle round an intruder calling loudly, trying to drive it away.

Bird-song is another form of courtship behaviour, and a male bird will sing, not only to prove his identity so that a female will recognise the songster as one of her own species, but also to proclaim a territory and warn off other birds. Many birds have favourite 'song-posts' and will sing every morning from the same vantage point on a tree, roof-top or even a television aerial. As the season advances, the songs of some birds become more complex, as 'practice makes perfect'. However, when the female has laid, the male usually stops singing, to avoid attracting the attention of predators to the nest.

NEST-BUILDING

All birds need to find a safe place to lay their eggs and rear their young; somewhere protected from extremes of heat or cold and as safe as possible from predators. Birds know instinctively how to build a nest, but even so, their nest-building ability can improve with practice. The variety of nests is as numerous and fascinating as the birds themselves. Some build immense, complicated structures, or weave small, intricate hanging nests. Others simply use holes in trees or dig them in riverbanks. Yet another group makes a simple scrape on the ground in which to lay their eggs.

Most tree holes are formed naturally. When a branch drops off, fungal decay eats into the tree, forming a hole which makes an ideal nesting-site for birds like starlings, parrots and owls. Other birds drill their own holes in decaying trees with their chisel-sharp bills.

Bee-eaters dig their burrows in riverbanks and sandbanks, using their long slender beaks as excavating tools. They will fly repeatedly beak-first at the face of a sandbank or cliff until they have made a small depression from which to hang. Thereafter the bird hammers away persistently until it has excavated a narrow tunnel as much as one metre long. Several species of bee-eater nest in huge colonies. One of them, the Red-throated Bee-eater of the savanna area, wisely digs its tunnel at the end of the rainy season when the ground is relatively soft, even though it will not be ready to lay its eggs for another three months. By nesting together bee-eaters are able to take advantage of the presence of young, unmated birds to assist in digging burrows and feeding nestlings. The colony also gives them greater protection from predators.

Hornbills nest in ready-made tree-holes but have developed a curious habit to protect the incubating female from predators. A large hole of the size needed by hornbills could easily be entered by predators like squirrels and snakes, so when the female begins to incubate the eggs, the male brings lumps of mud moistened with saliva to wall up the chamber, leaving only a tiny slit through which he can feed the entombed female. When the chicks are half-grown, the female will break out of the hole to assist her mate in the arduous task of feeding the ever-demanding family. Once the mother has left, the chicks rebuild the wall and remain sealed up until they are fully fledged and ready to fly.

The woodpecker chisels its own nest-hole out of a decaying tree-trunk, but sometimes finds that other creatures less well-equipped for hole construction, such as bats and squirrels, have taken it over so it has to begin all over again. Digging holes requires strength rather than ingenuity, but to construct a complicated nest of interlocking twigs requires great skill. Large birds of prey, like the Tawny Eagle, generally build bulky stick nests in the tops of tall trees, often adding to the same nest,

CARMINE BEE-EATER

GREY HORNBILL

year after year. The nest cup is lined with leaves to make a soft lining for the eggs and chicks. When the female settles down to incubate her eggs she carefully sheathes her huge talons to avoid breaking the eggs. When the chicks hatch, she tears off small strips of meat to feed to the chicks in an unexpectedly tender manner.

One of the largest nests in Africa is built by the strange-looking Hammerkop, so called because the crest on its head resembles the head of a hammer. It frequents swamps, rivers and mangrove creeks and builds a massive roofed structure of sticks, grass and mud in the fork of a tree, usually over water. Both birds take part in nest-building and it may reach a metre in height with a round entrance hole in one side. Sometimes nests are re-used for several years, and even provide a home for other species, particularly Barn Owls.

Doves also build stick nests but the nest is often so sparsely and untidily constructed that you can see daylight through it if you stand underneath. However, doves are one of the most successful species of bird in Nigeria, so possibly this roughly constructed nest, which despite its untidy appearance is made of carefully interlocked twigs, is less obvious to predators and so less frequently robbed than the nests of other birds.

In contrast with the comparatively simple nests of doves, weaver birds build complicated structures skilfully woven from strips of palm, creepers or grasses, and suspended from the tip of a branch. The various species of weaver in Nigeria construct different shaped nests, but they all use a technique similar to that of human weavers, creating cloth by weaving the threads in and out on a loom. Two basic skills are needed for this type of nest-building – knotting and weaving. The bird must start by making a knot to secure the nest to a small branch. It does this by holding down the strip with its foot and then, using its beak, passes it round the branch, threads it through one of the turns and pulls it tight. When the fastening is finished the bird begins weaving. Each strip is threaded beneath another one, which runs across it more or less at right angles and then pulled tight. Sometimes, if a strip is long enough, the bird will loop it back and weave in the opposite direction.

With these two basic skills, weavers can build a great variety of nests, some round, some domed and others with long entrance-tubes underneath to make it difficult for predators, especially snakes, to enter the nest. This weaving skill is obviously inherited as birds reared in an incubator are able to weave nests when they become adults, but there is much acquired skill involved too, as young male weavers, (it is always the male who builds the nest), often build badly constructed nests at the first attempt which are rejected by the female. When the nest is finished the male hangs upside down beneath it, fluttering his wings, inviting a female to inspect it. If it is not up to standard, he must start all over again.

Generally, weavers nest in colonies to give them greater security against predators. Many pairs of eyes are an advantage in spotting approaching danger. Some, like Village Weavers, prefer to nest in trees near buildings, as there is less danger from birds of prey so close to human beings. Others choose to make their nests in the branches of trees overhanging water, as this makes it more difficult for land predators such as the mongoose to reach the nests. The crafty Slender-billed Weaver often chooses a site near a wasps' nest, because strangely enough, the wasps do not bother the weavers, but will attack any other creature coming too close.

One of the most unusual nests is that of the Palm Swift, which is commonly found throughout Nigeria wherever there are palm trees. It constructs its nest on the underside of palm-fronds and the material it uses is almost entirely its own saliva, with the addition of a few feathers, moulded into a tiny spoon-shaped structure. To prevent the two eggs falling out, the swift glues them to the nest with more saliva, and incubates them in a vertical position. When the young hatch, they have to cling to the rim of the nest until they have developed sufficiently to fly. Surprisingly, this seemingly precarious nest has proved to be very successful.

Swallows build their nests with pellets of mud in much the same way that mud houses in Nigeria are built. Birds like the Rufous-breasted Swallow build their retort-shaped nests under roofs and bridges or in culverts. Here the nests will be sheltered from the heavy rain which would destroy them, as swallows breed in the wet season when they can readily obtain the mud from roadside puddles or beside waterholes. They pile the mud pellets on top of each other in the same way that human builders use mud bricks, leaving only a small entrance hole. When the mud hardens the nest is lined with grasses and feathers.

Sunbirds build delicate domed nests which are suspended from the tips of branches in small trees or shrubs. They generally use grasses and fibres stuck together with spider's webs and lined with feathers, but each species of sunbird has developed its own individual style. The nest of the Scarlet-breasted Sunbird, for example, has an untidy 'beard' of grasses hanging beneath it, but the Collared Sunbird makes a more compact nest altogether.

Birds which nest on the ground, such as plovers, often lay their eggs in a simple scrape. The Crocodile Bird, which nests on the sandbanks of the big rivers, has developed a very clever method of protecting its eggs and chicks. Whenever the bird leaves its nest, it covers the eggs by tossing sand over them with its bill. Throughout the day it carefully monitors the temperature of the eggs by testing the heat of the sand with its bill, and adjusts its behaviour accordingly. At night and in the early morning when the air is cool, the bird incubates the eggs itself, but in the mid-morning it leaves them covered with sand which will maintain the correct temperature for incubation. However, in the heat of the day the parent bird wets its feathers in the river every 15

CROCODILE BIRD

minutes or so, then returns to the nest to dampen the sand and shade the eggs in order to prevent them over-heating. When the chicks hatch, they too are covered with sand if the parent birds need to leave them to seek food, or if they sense danger nearby.

These few examples show a little of the infinite variety of nests built by African birds. It also illustrates the amazing ingenuity with which birds have adapted to their habitat in order to lay eggs and rear their chicks as safely as possible. Some birds, however, have been so little studied that we know next to nothing about their breeding behaviour.

Eggs and Chicks

All birds reproduce by laying hard-shelled eggs, and one or other of the parents must keep them at a constant temperature until they develop into chicks. They warm the eggs by pressing them against areas of bare skin on their breasts, called brood patches, which are usually concealed by feathers. If the eggs are allowed to cool once incubation has started, the developing chicks may die. Over-heating however, is also a danger, especially in Nigeria's hot climate, and we have already seen how the Crocodile Bird wets the eggs and shades them to keep them cool. Although a bird's instinct to keep its eggs at the correct temperature is very strong, human interference can easily cause birds to abandon their nests. If you discover a nest, avoid the temptation to keep on inspecting it or you will frighten the birds away.

The developing eggs must be turned frequently to prevent the unborn chick sticking to the membrane inside the egg, and the incubating bird does this with its bill. The incubation time varies from about ten days to several weeks, but generally the larger the bird, the longer the time it takes the eggs to hatch. When the chick is ready to hatch, it chips away at the shell with the eggtooth on the tip of its beak, and finally emerges into the world. The parent bird either removes the discarded egg-shells, flying some distance from the nest before dropping them, or in the case of birds like some plovers, eats the shells, to avoid drawing the attention of predators to the nestlings. Something else which would draw attention to the nest would be an accumulation of bird-droppings underneath it. To avoid this, some birds, especially song-birds, have developed a way to overcome it. The chick excretes its droppings in a neat little white sac, called a faecal sac, which the parent removes from the nest in its bill, and drops some distance away. Nesting time is a hazardous time for birds and their young, so these are very necessary precautions.

The amazing variety of birds and their nests is matched by the great variation in the size and colouring of their eggs. The largest egg of any living bird is that of the African Ostrich, which weighs up to 1.78 kg and has a volume equal to that of 24 hen's eggs! The egg is creamy white in colour and has a very tough shell. The smallest eggs in Africa are laid by tiny birds like the sunbirds, or the Yellow White-eye which lays a delicate pale blue egg, weighing only about 0.7 gm. In between these two extremes there are eggs of many different shapes and sizes. Basically most birds' eggs are oval and similar in shape to a hen's egg, but owls have much rounder eggs and others like Darters (or Snake-birds) lay eggs which taper to a point at one end to prevent them rolling out of the nest. Hole-nesters like woodpeckers, bee-eaters and kingfishers, usually lay white eggs as there is no need for colour in the darkness of a hole. Also, white eggs are easier for the parent birds to locate without breaking them.

Most other species lay beautifully patterned eggs in a variety of colours. The eggs of ground-nesting birds like plovers, thick-knees and snipe are camouflaged with blotches of browns and greens to help conceal them from predators.

There is also a great variation in clutch size. If predation rates are low, birds lay fewer eggs. Members of the pigeon family, for example, usually only lay two eggs. Most songbirds lay average-sized clutches of 3-5 but ground-nesting birds like Guinea-fowl where the young are at considerable risk from predators after hatching, lay clutches of up to 12 eggs to compensate for the high loss of chicks.

The chicks of these ground-nesting birds, such as the Spur-winged Plover, look wet and bedraggled when they hatch, but in a short time their feathers dry out to an attractive fluffy down, speckled like their eggs with 'earthy' colours. They are able to leave the nest within an hour or two, and run after the parents, but cannot fly, of course, until their adult feathers have grown. They can also feed themselves but the parents show them what to eat. You can see an example of this by studying a hen with her chickens. Watch how she scratches the ground with her feet to find food and then calls her chicks to come and eat. Chicks which are able to run away from the nest like this soon after hatching, are described as 'nidifugous'.

In some species like the Senegal Wattled Plover, the female will put on what is known as a 'distraction display'. She drags a wing and limps as if she is badly injured, to encourage a predator to follow her (but always keeping a safe distance ahead) to lead it away from her young. This dramatic act is so convincing, it is usually a very effective method of protecting helpless chicks.

Many species of songbirds, like bulbuls, sunbirds, finches and weavers build nests in trees and produce chicks that are naked, blind and helpless when they hatch. These are described as 'nidiculous' and must stay in the nest until their feathers have grown and they are able to fly. Before this has happened, the chicks are very vulnerable and need to grow fast and nature has given them a voracious appetite and a huge gape,

SPUR-WINGED PLOVER CHICK

SPUR-WINGED PLOVER

or mouth. The chicks stimulate their parents to feed them, by chirping impatiently and opening their gapes wide, which are often edged with yellow or red. The patterns inside the mouths of the chicks are very distinctive so that a bird can recognise the young of its own species. The parents begin feeding them at dawn and continue throughout most of the day, bringing caterpillars and insects continuously to their demanding infants.

When they are fully fledged (covered with feathers) they leave the nest, but often stay hidden in the leaves of a tree where their parents will continue to feed them until they are independent. This is the most dangerous time for the chicks, and many do not survive. However, if birds have one or more broods each season, with 5-6 chicks at a time, only two need to survive to keep the population constant. Cruel though it may seem, the 'harvest' of young birds is an important link in the food chain, as it provides food for birds of prey and land predators. As sick or weak chicks are more likely to be caught than the healthy ones, this helps to ensure that only the strongest birds survive to breed the following season.

Birds of prey, as well as owls, have developed a different pattern of behaviour for rearing their young. The eggs are laid at intervals of several days but the female begins incubating as soon as the first egg is laid. This means that the chicks hatch at intervals. Naturally, the oldest chick is the strongest and receives most of the food, so if prey is scarce and the male brings little to the nest, this chick is the only one to survive. The female instinctively feeds the most demanding chick and ignores the weaker one which may mean that the smaller chicks die, or are even killed by the firstborn and then eaten. If however, food is plentiful and the male can bring plenty of meat to the nest, when the largest chick is satisfied the female will then feed the next largest, so more than one chick will fledge. This behaviour seems cruel but it does ensure the continuation of the species. If the mother tried to feed all the chicks equally in times of scarcity, perhaps none of them would survive.

Young birds of prey are covered in white fluffy down when they hatch, but unlike the chicks of ground-nesting birds which are also covered in down, these young are blind and helpless and need the care of adults for several weeks and even months in the case of the large eagles. The male brings most of the food to the nest in the early days, when the female must guard the chicks. She tears off tiny strips of meat and feeds the chick tenderly until it is able to feed itself. Before leaving the nest, the chick must flap its wings from time to time to strengthen them. Even after it takes its first flight it may be fed by the parents for some time. However, hunting for prey is a skill which needs to be practised and when the parents finally leave the young birds to fend for themselves, some die because they cannot kill enough food to keep themselves alive.

One group of birds, however, manages to avoid most of the bother of nest-building and rearing its young. Cuckoos are 'parasitic' nesters, laying their eggs in the nests of other birds which rear their young for them. This is one of nature's most extraordinary stories.

The Didric Cuckoo is named after its distinctive call 'deea deea deedaric', and is possibly the commonest cuckoo in Nigeria, so we will study its behaviour in more depth. This cuckoo generally chooses weavers as its 'host'. After courtship and mating the female finds a weaver colony and observes it closely. When she identifies a nest with recently laid eggs, she waits in dense cover until the female weaver leaves the nest, then dashes in and lays an egg in a few seconds. The egg may have been ready in her body for at least a day, and has hardened to avoid breaking as it drops into the nest. She usually removes one of the host's eggs and then immediately flies off, although the weavers may mob her and even drive her to the ground. Sometimes the male assists by luring the weavers away and provoking an attack against himself, to allow the female a better chance to lay. She may lay as many as 16-21 eggs in different nests over a ten-week breeding season, and they will closely resemble the eggs of the host bird – if not, they will be rejected. For the female cuckoo this is the end of the story. However, for the chicks the battle for survival is just beginning.

The incubation period of cuckoos is short, only about 12 days, so the young cuckoo often hatches before the weaver's chicks. For the first two days of its life it has a strong instinct to remove either the eggs or other young from the nest. It does this by getting the egg or chick onto its own back then heaving it over the side of the nest. Now it can receive all the attention of the 'parent' weaverbirds who feed this large 'foundling' in their nest as if it was their own. It fledges after about three weeks, but the foster parents continue to feed it a little longer. Some observers think that young cuckoos are occasionally fed by adult cuckoos once they have left the nest, but this behaviour may have been courtship feeding of the female by the male. A few other birds beside cuckoos are parasitic nesters, such as the Pin-tailed and Broad-tailed Paradise Whydahs, but it is not a common behaviour pattern.

The plumage of young birds is often much duller than that of their parents, which helps to make them less conspicuous to predators but makes identification more difficult for the birdwatcher. The young Night Heron pictured here, with brownish-grey feathers blotched with white, looks very different from the smart grey and white adult with its distinctive black crown and back. Young birds of prey often retain their immature plumage for several years, for example, the Bateleur.

This brief description of the breeding behaviour of birds can only touch the surface of this fascinating subject. Every species of bird has its own particular breeding pattern which would take volumes to cover fully. However, there is still a great deal of fieldwork to be done on the breeding habits of many African birds, as there is much we do not know. This demands time and great patience during the hours of observation needed, but is a really exciting prospect for future ornithologists.

IMMATURE NIGHT HERON

The migration of birds is one of the wonders of nature and many of its secrets have yet to be revealed. For centuries no one knew where birds went to when they disappeared as the seasons changed. One celebrated eighteenth century British naturalist, Gilbert White, still considered that it was possible that swallows hibernated in underground burrows during the European winter!

We now know that some birds make incredibly long journeys from Africa, across thousands of kilometres, to nest in Europe and take advantage of the summer bonanza of small insects on which to feed their nestlings. They also benefit from the longer daylight hours, which give them more time to collect food for their ever-hungry nestlings, and from the smaller number of predators, as snakes in Africa account for the deaths of many young birds. When the European winter begins, insects die off or hibernate and are hard to find, so the birds must return to the warmth of Africa. Therefore, those wintering in Nigeria have to cross the inhospitable Sahara Desert twice a year.

There are also birds which migrate within Africa (intra-African migrants) such as the Abdim's Stork, which breeds in the wet season in the north of Nigeria, but migrates south of the Equator in the dry season. This stork is known by Hausa farmers as 'Shamuwa', the rain bird, as it is the harbinger of the rainy season. Its arrival tells farmers it is time to begin planting their crops. Others, like the White-throated Bee-eater, spend the dry season in the south of Nigeria but fly north to Niger to breed, passing through the savanna belt twice a year.

Much of the knowledge we have about migration is obtained from bird-ringing. Ornithologists either capture birds carefully in special nets, or find nestlings, and place small, numbered metal rings on their legs and then release them. If the bird is recaptured at a later date, the number on the ring is noted before re-releasing the bird, and the date and location compared with the original record. One Yellow Wagtail in Kano was retrapped after seven years, so it had crossed the Sahara at least 14 times already. Gulls and terns, however, being seabirds, travel round the coast of West Africa rather than flying over the desert.

How do birds find their way?

In making these long journeys, birds use almost every sense we know of and probably some we have not yet identified. Some birds navigate mainly by following geographic features such as river valleys and mountains. Some use the sun and stars and others use the earth's magnetic field to help them, but there is still a great deal that we do not understand about the ability of a bird to navigate so accurately. Swallows, for example, can find their way back to exactly the same barn in which they had hatched the previous year, after a journey of thousands of kilometres. Some birds though, seem to know instinctively how to find their way. Young cuckoos leave Europe for Africa later than their parents so they have no one to guide them, yet the majority of them arrive safely.

It is a most hazardous journey, however, as there are many dangers along the route. Many birds travel by night, so that they can see the stars, but if the night is cloudy they must wait until conditions are right again, or risk losing their way. Before

BIRD MIGRATION ROUTES

migrating, birds eat large quantities of food to build up their body weight to provide reserves of energy for the long journey ahead.

From Nigeria the first major obstacle for birds travelling northwards in March and April is the Sahara Desert. If the oases they use as stopping places to replenish themselves with food and water have dried out, then many birds do not survive the journey. Sandstorms can also take a terrible toll of migrating birds. The next danger they encounter is when they reach the shores of the Mediterranean where hunters are waiting to shoot the arriving birds, in spite of intense pressure being put on these countries to give up this destructive practice.

For those who survive the journey so far, the next hurdle is the huge mountain ranges of the Alps and the Pyrenees. Storms and cold weather can prove fatal for the weakened birds, but for those who reach their destination safely the rewards are great, as food and water are plentiful. The birds quickly set about establishing a territory and finding a mate and nest-building follows immediately. Some small birds even have time for two broods before the whole journey must begin again in reverse. In September and October as the days begin to shorten, they set off for the warmth of Africa once again. To illustrate the story of migration, let us follow two completely different birds on their journeys.

The Story of the White Stork

The life story of the White Stork begins in Western Europe for this is where the birds that spend the dry season in Nigeria go to breed. The young storks are hatched in huge nests made of twigs, often on the roofs of houses and farm buildings in villages in Spain. Their parents feed them on frogs and small rodents, such as fieldmice and voles, from the marshes and farmlands around the villages, until they are strong enough to leave the nest. Before they make their first tentative flight, however, they spend a great deal of time exercising their wings by flapping them vigorously. Finally they pluck up courage to leave the nest and are soon feeding in the fields and marshes alongside their parents to gain enough weight for their long journey to Nigeria.

As the days begin to shorten the birds become restless and start gathering on the rooftops. Finally, in September, the time comes for them to set off for Africa, an exhausting and hazardous journey of thousand of kilometres which will take them about four weeks. Storks stop at night to rest and may spend a day or two on the way to feed, 'refuelling' themselves for the next stage. They normally travel at a speed of about 35 km per hour but with a following wind they can glide at speeds of up to 80 km per hour. Storks fly by using the rising air currents, called thermals, to lift them into the air from where they can glide from one thermal to another, so minimising the effort required for flight. Flapping-flight is much more costly in terms of energy needed.

Their journey takes them through Spain to cross the Mediterranean Sea by one of the shortest routes, the Straits of Gibraltar. If they cross the Mediterranean safely, they then face the dangerous journey across the Sahara, where sandstorms and the thick dust of the harmattan can seriously delay them. Eventually, the surviving birds reach the relative safety of places like the Hadejia Wetlands and the Dagona Wildfowl Reserve in Borno State. Here they can spend the next few months building up their reserves of energy for the equally testing journey back to their nesting grounds in

Western Europe next spring. Sadly, the White Stork which has lived in close proximity with human beings for centuries, is now in decline. In Chapter Ten we will discuss the threats which face these elegant black and white birds and the measures that need to be taken to protect them.

(Adapted from the Royal Society for the Protection of Birds video called 'The Year of the Stork', narrated by Sir David Attenborough.)

The Story of the Willow Warbler

In contrast with the large White Stork, the Willow Warbler is a tiny bird weighing a mere nine grams, but this bird too, can undertake the long journey from Europe to Nigeria. It is almost unbelievable that such a small creature can fly such huge distances, which for a human being would be the equivalent of a journey to the moon and back five times.

This time the story begins in England, where the young Willow Warbler has hatched in the spring and spent the warm summer exploring the surrounding woodlands. As the cold weather approaches the bird grows increasingly restless until finally it obeys the strong urge to begin its journey. One night in August, instead of going to roost, it ascends a hundred metres or so into the darkening sky and heads south. Its destination is Africa, a far off land that it has never seen, and its only guide is an instinctive set of instructions programmed into its genes over thousands of generations, aided by a substance in its head which is sensitive to the earth's magnetic field. As it flies it notes major landmarks which help it to build up a mental map of its route which will assist it to navigate on the return journey. As it flies through the night sky it is aware of other birds migrating south, as their calls break the silence of the night. Before dawn the bird will descend to a patch of woodland to rest and feed. As the weeks proceed, the warbler will follow the routine of flying south by night and resting and feeding by day, taking advantage as much as possible, of the winds blowing from the north to assist it on its way.

The first major hazard it will meet is a broad expanse of sea, the English Channel. To begin with, the Willow Warbler may hesitate, and fly up and down the coast, but eventually the urge to fly south overcomes its reluctance and if the night is clear, it will head out across the sea. Soon it will reach the coast of France and then continue south over Spain. Again it must cross the sea, but this time the Mediterranean, where danger threatens in the form of hunting packs of Eleanora's Falcons, birds of prey that specialise in catching small songbirds on migration. Once safely in North Africa it will spend several days refuelling for the rigours of the journey across the Sahara. With luck it will find an oasis en route where it can rest and feed, but it must be prepared to do the whole journey in one stretch, flying day and night over the barren sand. Once it reaches the border of Nigeria it will fly further south until it finds a suitable woodland where insects are abundant, and here it will settle for the next few months, feeding to build up its strength until once more the urge to migrate overwhelms it. This time, of course, the direction will be north.

(Adapted from the RSPB magazine 'Birds', Autumn 1990.)

Chapter Three

THE CLIMATE AND VEGETATION ZONES OF NIGERIA

As we have seen in the previous chapter, the distribution of birds is closely related to their habitat. Some birds have become adapted to living in tropical rainforests, and others in arid zones, for example. Therefore, to know where different species of birds are likely to be found in Nigeria, it is necessary to study the climate and vegetation.

Because of the vast size of the country there are great changes in the vegetation from north to south. Climatic changes, and in particular the decreasing amount of rainfall, are the main cause of this transition from moist tropical forest in the south through the savannas of the middle belt to the arid thornscrub of the north. Man too, has also had a major impact on the vegetation of the country.

However, it should be noted that some birds are very adaptable, for example, the Common Garden Bulbul, which is found almost throughout the country. Others, like forest or montane species are much more closely tied to their own specialised habitats.

CLIMATE

Nigeria lies in the tropical belt between approximately 4° and 13° north of the Equator. The climate is largely determined by the seasonal movements of the prevailing winds. In the months of April to October these winds blow from the south-west, bringing moist weather from the Atlantic Ocean. Then from October to April the prevailing winds are from the north-east, bringing the arid, dusty winds from the Sahara known as the Harmattan. This results in two main seasons, the wet season and the dry season, but as the moisture produced by the south-westerly winds falls mainly in the south, the wet season is longer in the south and grows progressively shorter towards the north, resulting in drier and more arid conditions. The annual rainfall varies from over 155 cm in the south to less than 50 cm in the extreme north. The south experiences a much higher level of humidity too, which keeps the temperature more constant, whereas the north is drier with less cloud cover. This causes more marked seasonal temperature changes north of the great rivers, with much cooler weather during the Harmattan period around December and January and considerably hotter weather during April and May, before the rains begin.

Being so close to the Equator, there is little change in day-length throughout the year although there is some increase from south to north. In Lagos there is only 35 minutes difference between the longest day in June and the shortest day in December, whereas in Katsina or Maiduguri for example, the difference is as much as 90 minutes.

This brief description of the climate of Nigeria can only give a very general picture. However, it provides a basic framework for understanding the changes in vegetation throughout the length of the country and the way this affects the distribution of bird species. There are naturally slight variations in climate within this overall pattern, and often noticeable changes from year to year, especially as much of the rain falls in sudden localised storms. Unfortunately the north has been experiencing drought conditions throughout the 1970s and 80s with the consequent lowering of the water-table and the threat of increasing desertification.

VEGETATION ZONES

Beginning at the coast and travelling north to the border with the country of Niger, one finds that the vegetation of Nigeria can be divided broadly into five zones. Then, in the Obudu and Mambilla Plateaux in the east, there is a distinct montane (or mountain-type) vegetation, making a total of six zones. These are:

1. Coastal mangrove and swamp forest
2. Rainforest and derived savanna
3. Guinea Savanna
4. Sudan Savanna
5. Sahel Savanna
6. Montane (mountain forest and grasslands)

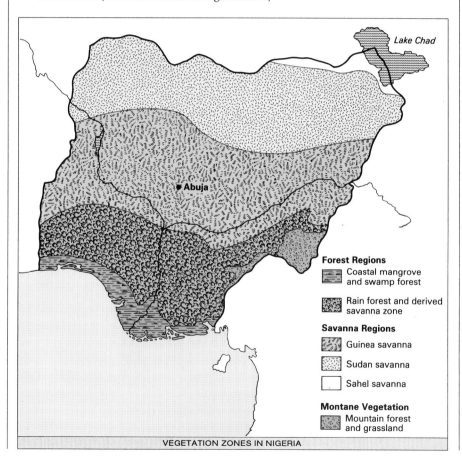

VEGETATION ZONES IN NIGERIA

Coastal Mangrove and Swamp Forest

The coast of Nigeria is dominated by the Niger Delta, a maze of tidal creeks and lagoons reaching up to 50 km inland. This system of waterways spreads along the entire coastline from Badagri to Calabar, but only extends so far inland in the delta area. The lagoons and creeks are bordered by red mangrove, which can reach a height of 40 m. Away from the creek edges the main plant is the white mangrove, which grows to a maximum of 30 m. Mangrove trees are specially adapted to living in an estuarine environment as they are resistant to the effects of salt water, and have developed aerial roots which not only support them but have the ability to obtain oxygen from the air.

Because the mud makes it impossible to travel on foot and the only access to these areas is by boat, the birdlife of the mangroves has been little explored. Large water-birds like the Little Egret, Green-backed Heron and Hammerkop are conspicuous while the huge stick nests of the Hammerkop can sometimes be seen in mangrove trees along the edge. It is more difficult to spot the smaller non-aquatic birds that live along the fringes of the creeks, such as the Moho, Scarlet-spectacled Wattle-eye and Blue-breasted Kingfisher, which are more often heard than seen. In the dry season waders like Whimbrels and Common Sandpipers feed on the mudflats at low tide.

Along the ocean-facing sandy shores of the coastline, where the beaches are steep and the wave action fierce, there are few birds to be seen. Yet where there are shallower beaches, such as Lighthouse Beach near Tarkwa Bay off Lagos, many seabirds and small waders like Sanderlings and White-fronted Sand-plovers can be seen. Lesser Black-backed Gulls and several varieties of tern are a common sight in Lagos Harbour.

Inland from the coastal mangroves lies a belt of freshwater swamp forest, which is at its widest in the Niger Delta area, where it stretches inland for nearly 100 km. The vegetation is a mixture of raphia palm and forest trees reaching a height of about 30 m. Here there are a great variety of both waterbirds and forest birds. Pairs of

COASTAL MANGROVES NEAR LAGOS

Hartlaub's Duck, which can be identified in flight by the blue wing patch, frequent the freshwater creeks. Where there is floating vegetation, Lily-trotters can be seen picking their way across the flat leaves. Along the edges Malachite Kingfishers can sometimes be spotted perched silently over the water, and flocks of Swamp-palm Bulbuls babble noisily in the raphia palms. In the trees behind, forest birds like Black-and-white-tailed Hornbills and Green Fruit-pigeons are a common sight. It is interesting to explore this area by boat along the freshwater creeks, although forest birds are more often heard than seen in the dense cover, and waterbirds like crakes and rails are especially secretive, so it requires a quiet and patient approach.

Rainforest and Derived Savanna

Although rainforest once covered a broad belt across the whole of southern Nigeria, there are now only patches of it left. These are mostly confined to places like Okomu Forest Reserve in Edo State and the Oban Hills in Cross River State. Much of the high forest has been cut down to make way for plantations of oil-palm, rubber, cocoa and fast-growing exotic trees for pulp and plywood. Derived savanna now occurs where the forest was felled for farming and then abandoned when the soil became exhausted, leaving patches of savanna-like land with smaller trees, shrubs and grassy clearings.

The crowning glories of the rainforest are the tall hardwood timber trees for which Nigeria used to be famous, like the African mahogany, iroko or Sapele. Unfortunately it is chiefly the demand for these trees that has led to so much destruction of the forest. Hardwood trees can reach a height of 60 m and their leafy crowns tower over the forest. Their trunks are straight and free of branches, while at the base many of these trees form strong buttresses to support their weight in the shallow forest soil. Beneath these tallest trees there are smaller ones which help to create the continuous forest canopy. Below this there is an understorey of small trees and shrubs, but because of the small amount of light reaching the forest floor, there is little ground cover and grasses are almost absent. In fact the presence of ground cover in a forest is an

RAINFOREST - KWA FALLS, CROSS RIVER STATE

indication of disturbance, as it is only when trees are removed that the increased light allows it to develop. A variety of ferns and orchids grow from the branches of trees at all heights, with lianas and vines hanging down in tangled masses, adding to the complexity of the plant species.

The rainforest provides habitat for about 200 bird species. It is able to support this number because most of these species show preference for a particular level of the forest. In other words, they each occupy a different ecological niche. Spectacular birds like the Brown-cheeked Hornbill and the huge, brightly coloured Blue Plantain-eater, which are mainly fruit-eating, inhabit the canopies of the trees. African Grey Parrots and Green Fruit-pigeons also prefer the higher levels. In the lower strata of the forest are many species of barbets, bulbuls, flycatchers, warblers and sunbirds, and close to ground level are Forest Robins and other small birds. In the early mornings the rainforest is full of birdsong and calls. The birds need to communicate with each other by sound because the thickness of the undergrowth prevents much visual communication. Forest birds are difficult to see because of the dense vegetation, but to listen to the chorus of birdsong in the mornings is an exciting experience it itself. This is a rich and unique habitat which contains many animal species, especially monkeys, as well as birds.

Tropical rainforest is the most complex of all plant communities, because of the huge number of species it contains. Unfortunately, because of this it is also the most vulnerable. Once it has been destroyed it is impossible to recreate an identical tree cover, because much of the fertility will have been leached away by the heavy rainfall and some of the species may have become extinct. Although if left undisturbed a new climax vegetation, or secondary forest, will develop in time. However, as it takes about 200 years for a giant forest tree to reach its full height, the re-establishment of forest would take centuries. Much of the remnant forest in the south-west of Nigeria is, in fact, secondary forest, due to intensive human occupation in the past.

Therefore, the importance of preserving the rainforest cannot be over-estimated, both for its regulatory effect on the climate of the entire planet and its potential as a genetic storehouse for the medicines and agricultural products of the future. Only recently scientists discovered a powerful new drug through observing wild chimpanzees selecting 'medicinal' plants in the forest when suffering from stomach upsets. It is vital that the rainforest is preserved for future generations to enjoy too, although sadly, in many areas it is already too late. The Cross River National Park is the last remaining area of totally undisturbed primary rainforest left in Nigeria and every effort must be made to ensure its survival.

Derived savanna has now taken the place of rainforest in a broad band north of the remaining forest and in many areas of the south where the forest has been felled. Unfortunately, the great misconception is that because the vegetation of the rainforest is so rich in species, the soil must be extremely fertile and once cleared the land would be excellent for farming. In fact, all the nutrients are stored in the forest canopy and once the trees are felled the fertility of the soil is quickly leached away by the heavy rainfall, so the land only remains fertile for the growing of cassava, yams and maize for about five years. It is then abandoned, allowing the land to become a mixture of secondary forest and savanna-like areas. These areas are then colonised by birds normally found only in the true savanna, like the Grey Hornbill, Pin-tailed Whydah and the White-fronted Black-chat. The presence of these birds provides evidence of the changing nature of the habitat.

Guinea (Woodland) Savanna

This type of savanna is characterised by broadleaved woodland with trees 13-17 m high, and grassy cover in between. It stretches from just south of the great rivers, the Niger and Benue, to roughly Zaria and Bauchi in the north. In the wet season the grass grows to between one and two metres in height but is often deliberately burnt by farmers in the dry season, to encourage the new growth. The trees are mainly fire-tolerant as the savannas have evolved because of the natural fires caused by lightning. Although the trees are able to withstand fires early in the dry season, late dry season fires which are a great deal hotter, can kill many of the trees. Combined with low rainfall and a lowering water table, this can dramatically alter the form of the tree cover, and farmers should be made aware of this danger. Two of the larger trees are the Shea-butter tree and the Locust-bean, but as one proceeds northwards, the trees become sparser and the grassland more open. The presence of tsetse fly has kept the human population relatively low, and much of the land is still covered with natural vegetation. The landscape is dotted with rocky outcrops, or inselbergs. These often have a more specialised bird population, with species like the Cinnamon-breasted Rock Bunting, White-crowned Cliff-chat, Fox Kestrel and the Freckled Nightjar, which lays its eggs in a depression on the bare rock.

The more open landscape of the Guinea savanna provides suitable habitat for birds which feed mainly on large insects, like the Abyssinian Roller and the Grasshopper Buzzard. The Red-throated Bee-eater is the commonest bee-eater of the savanna, where there are riverbanks for its nesting colonies. The Red and Fire-crowned Bishops are found where there are cornfields, and seed-eating finches like the Senegal Fire-finch and Red-cheeked Cordon-Bleu are familiar birds of the garden compound. The Purple Glossy Starling is the most numerous starling in the middle

GUINEA SAVANNA - YANKARI, BAUCHI STATE

belt of Nigeria and the Vinaceous Dove the most plentiful dove. Birds of prey like the Red-tailed Buzzard and Black-shouldered Kite are relatively common as they can spot their prey easily in the open grassland. It is also easier for the birdwatcher to spot birds here rather than in the dense foliage of the forest, especially in the dry season when many of the savanna trees have shed their leaves.

The great rivers, the Niger and the Benue, traverse the whole of this area, with their confluence at Lokoja, and provide a habitat for many waterside birds, such as plovers and waders. At the beginning of the rains, thousands of Rosy Bee-eaters congregate at selected places on these rivers. Here they form their breeding colonies and dig their nest-burrows in the sandbanks before these are covered by water later on in the rains.

Sudan (Dry) Savanna

The Guinea Savanna merges into the drier, more open Sudan savanna north of a line roughly level with Zaria and Bauchi. This area is heavily populated and much of it is farmed in spite of a 7-8 month dry season. Here the natural vegetation changes gradually from broadleaf trees to thorny species such as acacia, and the huge gnarled baobab tree is common around villages. The grass cover grows to barely a metre and in the north of the area the presence of the dum-palm, with its branching stems, is an indication of the increasing dryness of the climate.

Here the Blue-eared Glossy Starling is the commonest starling, although the handsome Chestnut-bellied Starling is probably more conspicuous in farmland areas. The slender Long-tailed Dove, with its black-faced male and duller female, becomes more abundant as one travels north. The huge communal nests of the Buffalo Weaver, looking like bundles of hay in the trees, are a familiar sight in northern cities like Kano. Dark Chanting Goshawks are frequently seen perching on trees or telegraph posts beside the roads. The Little Green Bee-eater favours this part of the country too, and huge flocks of weavers and Queleas feed on the millet and other grains which are

SUDAN SAVANNA

grown in such large quantities in this region.

This dry part of Nigeria, however, contains the western shores of Lake Chad and the Hadejia wetlands, an extensive inland drainage area which is home to thousands of waterbirds, especially in the dry season when the numbers are swelled by millions of Palearctic migrants. It is one of the most important areas for birds in Nigeria, as well as for the farmers who benefit from the water for their crops. As the waters recede at the beginning of the dry season, the crops are planted in the fertile soils that are exposed, and are harvested before the rains fill up the wetlands once again.

Sahel Savanna

This arid region is confined to a small area in the north of the country, in Jigawa, Yobe and Borno States. However, it is increasing in size as desertification of the area continues because of the felling of trees for firewood, the overgrazing by sheep, goats and cattle, and the frequent incidence of drought. The vegetation is a mixture of spiky thornbushes and grasses, with increasing numbers of windblown sand-dunes, interrupted in places by the occasional oasis encircled by dum-palms. The sparse, flat-topped trees, mainly acacia, are patchily distributed and only reach a height of about seven metres.

Around waterholes the bright yellow Sudan Golden Sparrow and the farmer's enemy, the Quelea, can be seen in flocks, and the delicately coloured Rose-grey Dove is not uncommon. Resident in this semi-desert area are Great Grey Shrikes, which sit conspicuously on top of thorn-bushes. Dull-coloured Ant-chats can also be seen, mostly in small flocks, rising from the ground around termite mounds, revealing the flash of white on their wings in flight. An indication of the southward march of the Sahara is the recent appearance of more typical desert species usually only found north of Nigeria's border, like the Cream-coloured Courser and the White-fronted Finch-Lark. Once again, birds have alerted us to a serious threat to the ecology of an area.

SAHEL SAVANNA

MONTANE FOREST - OBUDU HILLS, CROSS RIVER STATE

Montane forest and grassland

Montane (or mountain) forest and grassland only occur on the Obudu and Mambilla Plateaux in Nigeria. Montane forest, above an altitude of 1650 m, is very different from lowland forest. Because of the high humidity and lower temperatures for much of the year, there are days when the trees are shrouded in mist, giving it its more appropriate name of 'mist forest'. The trees are only 15-25 m in height and as their canopies are not dense enough to exclude the light, there is a variety of thick vegetation at ground level, including tree ferns. The trunks of many trees are covered with epiphytes (such as orchids) and large mosses but with few lianas in comparison to lowland rainforest. Most of the forest lies in valleys, whilst grassy tussocks with some low shrubby plants and brackens form the ground cover of the hilltops.

The more temperate climate of these montane areas means that there are many birds on the plateaux which are found nowhere else in Nigeria. Two examples are the Grey-throated Bulbul and Gilbert's Babbler, which live in the forest. In the grassland areas the only bee-eater is the Blue-breasted, which can be mistaken for the Little Bee-eater but has a blue chestband instead of black. Stonechats, which are resident here, are usually confined to temperate regions. The distinctive black, white and brown males can be seen in the breeding season perching conspicuously on tall grassy stems. The Black-crowned Waxbill is the common small finch both at the Obudu Cattle Ranch and on the Mambilla Plateau. The Olive Pigeon and Mackinnon's Shrike are two birds which are only seen in the Obudu area and because of the restricted habitat, like many of these montane birds, they are endangered species.

CONCLUSION

This brief description has illustrated the enormous range in climate and vegetation from the coastal swamps to the borders of the desert, which makes up this vast country of Nigeria. It has also attempted to explain why there is such a diversity of bird species, over 840 in all, including both resident and migrant birds. It has shown too, that birds are excellent indicators of the state of the habitat and important factors in the maintenance of bio-diversity. Ultimately bird conservation is also crucial for future human survival. It is important to preserve the habitat of the country, not only for the continuation of the bird species, but also for the benefit of the human population, whose farming practices must be adapted to maintain the ecological richness of the country.

Chapter Four

BIRDS OF THE GARDEN AND COMPOUND

The birds we see most often are obviously those which choose to live beside us in our gardens and compounds. The best way to begin birdwatching is by observing these common birds, especially if you encourage them by growing trees and flowering shrubs in your compound, and putting out water in a shallow earthenware dish for them to drink and bathe. Small finches like Senegal Fire-finches can become quite tame in the presence of humans and Bronze Mannikins even nest in bushes on the balconies of tower blocks in Lagos suburbs. Sunbirds are attracted to compounds with flowers where they can find nectar, whilst starlings and Grey-headed Sparrows are constant visitors to the bird bath. The Shikra, a small grey bird of prey, also benefits from living close to human-beings as these birds often snatch lizards from the walls of houses. The following is a small selection of the common birds seen in gardens and compounds in Nigeria.

SENEGAL KINGFISHER

The Senegal Kingfisher is one of Nigeria's most colourful and conspicuous birds, but despite the name 'kingfisher' it is mainly insectivorous, so is usually found away from water. It is a familiar bird in the compounds of Ikoyi and Victoria Island in Lagos and

SENEGAL KINGFISHER

is resident all the year round in the extreme south, but during the rains there is a definite movement into northern areas. It is a medium-sized kingfisher, with a grey head and underparts and conspicuous azure-blue and black wings and back. The large upper mandible is red and the lower, black. The Senegal Kingfisher often has favourite perches, such as a particular branch or a telegraph wire, from which to spot insects before diving down to seize them. Its sharp, rattling call is very noticeable in the breeding season, when the birds display by standing erect facing each other, opening and closing their wings like enormous butterflies. Unlike the true 'fishing' kingfishers, the Senegal Kingfisher nests in tree holes and even in holes under the roofs of houses, so is quite at home in suburban gardens, and is not particularly shy.

RED-EYED DOVE

The Red-eyed Dove is common in the south but becomes progressively less common northwards. Although it is also a bird of the woodlands, it is a familiar bird in Lagos compounds and is easily distinguished from the smaller Laughing Dove by its larger size and the conspicuous black half-collar on its neck. Its plumage is more uniformly brown in colour, with vinous (wine-coloured) underparts and a bluey-grey head. The absence of white in its tail feathers also helps to distinguish it from the Laughing Dove, although the tips of its tail feathers are paler, and there is a broad black band at the base of the tail. The call of the Red-eyed Dove is very distinctive and the series of notes, 'coo COO coo coo-coo-coo' can most easily be remembered by the phrase 'Avoid calamity'. It also makes a mewing sound when it alights on a tree. The male displays to the female by ascending with a loud clapping flight and then glides down on outstretched wings, or by a 'bowing' display, when he inflates his throat and bobs up and down, making a throaty, cooing sound. They build simple stick nests in the fork of a branch and although they breed throughout much of the year, the main breeding season is at the beginning of the rains. Like all other pigeons, they lay two white eggs and the young (squabs) are fed on regurgitated 'pigeon milk', a rich secretion of the crop made by both parents.

SENEGAL COUCAL

The Senegal Coucal, although widespread and found in a variety of habitats, is commonly seen in compounds with trees and bushes providing plenty of cover. A medium large bird with a longish tail, it is more often heard than seen. The coucal is a handsome bird with black head and tail, reddish-brown back and whitish underparts. Some coucals have black underparts and these 'melanics' were thought to be a different species. These dark birds are numerous near Lagos but do not occur in the dry north. The reddish eye is clearly visible when seen at close quarters. It tends to skulk in the undergrowth but its low, musical call, like the sound of water bubbling out of a bottle, often betrays its presence. The Coucal's flight is weak and it never flies far, often landing clumsily as if it has lost its balance. This is reflected in the Hausa names of 'Ragon maza' or 'Dan Ragua', meaning 'The Lazy People', and is the theme of the African fable in Chapter Eleven. The nest is a large domed structure near the ground, usually well concealed in a thick bush.

RED-EYED DOVE

SENEGAL COUCAL

YELLOW WAGTAIL

Unlike the resident black and white African Pied Wagtail, the Yellow Wagtail is a dry season migrant to Nigeria. These active little birds with bright yellow underparts are found in areas where the grass is short, throughout the country, during this season, so often frequent gardens and playing fields. Yellow Wagtails spend much of the day in small flocks, stalking purposefully across the grass, wagging their long tails and darting energetically after insects. Besides gardens, they are also seen on farmland, especially where there are grazing animals, and often near water.

WEST AFRICAN THRUSH

Another bird which feeds mainly on the ground is the West African Thrush, which frequents suburban gardens, where it feeds mainly on worms, snails, insects and also berries. It is common from the coast northwards, but absent in the far north, although during the rains some birds migrate northwards to the drier areas. It is a medium-sized bird with dull brownish plumage, paler underparts and brownish flecks on the throat. The rusty-coloured flanks can be seen when the bird flies, and the yellow bill is conspicuous in the adult. When feeding on the ground, it inclines its head to help it judge the distance to its prey more accurately, then runs forward to seize the insect or worm. Its alarm call is a sharp 'tchuck, tchuck, tchuck'. It breeds chiefly in the rains when its melodious song, with repetitive phrases, is heard. The largish cup-shaped nest, made of roots and grasses, is built in the fork of a tree and lined with fine fibre. The eggs are a pale bluish-green, freckled all over with reddish-brown spots.

VILLAGE WEAVER

The Village Weaver is the commonest weaver in towns and gardens throughout Nigeria. The lives of this weaver are centred around the breeding colony and they often nest in large trees close to houses in order to gain protection from predators. In many parts of Nigeria it is thought to be lucky to have a colony in the compound. In the breeding season the male has a black head and a distinctive V-shaped marking across its back and most of the rest of the plumage is golden yellow. The female, and the male in 'eclipse' plumage, (non-breeding) is mottled olive-green above and dull yellow below, without the black head. The nesting habits of the Village Weaver have been fully described in Chapter Two, but it is worth noting that they sometimes nest in mixed colonies with Chestnut-and-black Weavers.

YELLOW WHITE-EYE

The tiny Yellow White-eye is a common resident in gardens from the savanna to the coast. These little birds with yellowish-green upperparts and bright yellow underparts, are often seen in parties, searching actively for insects among the leaves of trees and shrubs with their sharp black bills. The constant squeaking call helps to keep the birds together as they feed. The most distinctive feature is the ring of white feathers round the eye, which gives them their common name. The White-eye's nest is a tiny woven cup suspended between two twigs, and two or three pale blue eggs are laid.

YELLOW WAGTAIL

WEST AFRICAN THRUSH

VILLAGE WEAVER

YELLOW WHITE-EYE

Chapter Five

BIRDS OF THE WATER AND WATERSIDE

The description 'waterbirds' is used here as a general term to include both the true waterbirds like ducks, herons and lily-trotters, but also the kingfishers, waders and other birds which live near water, like several members of the plover family. This group includes some of the best known and most conspicuous birds in Nigeria. However, there are many different types of waterside habitat, varying from the coastal mangrove swamps, the narrow bush clad rivers of the forest zone, the wide sandbanks of the great rivers and the wetlands of the arid north. Some birds, like the Malachite Kingfisher, White-faced Tree-duck and the Little Egret are widely distributed throughout the country, but others are restricted to more localised habitats. There are many species of waterbirds in Nigeria, but the following birds are some of the most familiar.

HERONS AND EGRETS

The graceful Little Egret is a relatively common bird throughout all types of wetland in Nigeria, especially in the dry season when the numbers are increased by birds migrating south from Europe. It can be confused with other white egrets though, but the Great White Egret is considerably larger and the smaller Cattle Egret is often seen

LITTLE EGRET

some distance from water. The Little Egret has a slender black bill and black legs with conspicuous yellow feet, unlike the Cattle Egret which has a yellow bill and legs. The Little Egret is always found near water, where it feeds by wading in the shallows, darting nimbly after fish and aquatic insects. These egrets are usually solitary, rather than in small flocks like the Cattle Egret. However, they congregate every evening at their roost on trees overlooking water. Sometimes the trees can turn white with the egrets' droppings, which may eventually kill off the tree. Although the Little Egret feeds chiefly by walking in the water, it sometimes deliberately disturbs the mud with its feet to flush out prey. It is a familiar bird in the coastal marshes near Lagos in the dry season. When the marshes are drying out, the egrets are forced to congregate in the same feeding area, and can sometimes be quite aggressive, chasing a rival away with a raucous croak.

The Squacco Heron is smaller and more thickset than the Little Egret and has shorter legs. It is also both a resident and a migrant and is more common in the north of the country, although it is sometimes seen in quite large numbers at the International Institute for Tropical Agriculture (IITA) in Ibadan. This is the bird which does a 'disappearing act' when it lands. Although it seems completely white in flight, it is actually only the wings that are white. When these are closed on landing, it becomes an inconspicuous brown-streaked bird which blends perfectly with its background. In the breeding season, the Squacco Heron has a cascade of plumes down its back. It uses a different method of hunting from the Little Egret, as it crouches almost horizontally in a concealed position in reedbeds and amongst pondweed, stalking insects, fish or frogs, and catching them with a swift jab. It gets its name from its sharp squawking call.

The Green-backed Heron, with its blackish, elongated crest, is a short stocky bird that appears dark grey rather than green. However, in certain lights it is possible to see the greenish tinge of the feathers on its back. Although a handsome little heron,

SQUACCO HERON

it is partly nocturnal and often only glimpsed as a small dark bird with orange-yellow feet as it flies off. During the day it hides in a concealed position in marshes or rice paddies and does not like disturbance. At close range it is possible to see the dark head and the brown markings on the front of its neck, outlined against the grey throat. The female Green-backed Heron builds a flimsy stick nest in thick vegetation usually a metre or so above water. The male brings the sticks to the female and the nest is completed in about three days.

The Hammerkop is a curious bird only found in Africa. It is related to the heron family and always found near water. A plain brown bird with a distinctive shaggy crest and stout black bill, it frequents swamps, rice paddies, riverside pools and mangrove swamps. In Nigeria Hammerkops are more common in the Niger delta area and in waterside habitats in the savanna, north of the great rivers. This bird was photographed at Yankari Game Reserve where it was feeding in a large puddle near the Gaji River, stirring the water with its foot to flush out prey. The Hammerkop builds a huge roofed nest in a tree beside water, and this is described in more detail in the section on nests in Chapter Two.

STORKS AND IBISES

The largest stork found in Nigeria is the Saddlebill Stork a huge, striking black and white bird standing nearly one metre tall. Its name comes from the curious yellow 'saddle' on its massive red and black bill. The long legs are black with red joints. Unfortunately it is not at all common, but at least one pair lives in the marshes of the Gaji river at Yankari and is regularly seen by visitors to the Game Reserve. It feeds mainly on fish and frogs and stalks its prey like a heron. In the air it is a majestic sight as it soars to a great height with its neck out-stretched and feet protruding beyond the tail.

The Wood Ibis, whose alternative name is the Yellow-billed Stork as it is in fact a stork, rather than an ibis, is much smaller than the Saddlebill Stork. Small flocks are often seen in the northern wetlands, usually in the company of other storks or spoonbills. It has a slightly curved yellow bill and the bare patch of skin on its face becomes red in the breeding season. Although mainly a black and white stork, close to, the pinkish tinge to its white feathers is clearly visible. The first-year stork is mainly greyish-brown. When resting, the Wood Ibis often squats with its legs folded underneath it, as is shown in the photograph. This stork breeds in northern Nigeria and nests in colonies, building a stick nest in a tall tree like a baobab, sometimes in villages.

The Glossy Ibis is a slender medium-sized wading bird with a long down-curved bill which it uses to probe the mud for its food, like the birds in the photograph. Although this ibis appears uniformly dark at a distance, close to, both the bronzy-green sheen on its brown plumage and the white spots on its head and neck are visible. The Glossy Ibis is a dry season migrant to Nigeria when it is commonly seen in the northern wetlands and is a gregarious bird, usually found in small flocks wading at the edge of marshes. It can be confused with the much larger Hadada Ibis which is resident all the year in Nigeria, but the Hadada has a white stripe on its cheek and a loud, raucous call.

GREEN-BACKED HERON

HAMMERKOP

SADDLEBILL STORK

WOOD IBIS

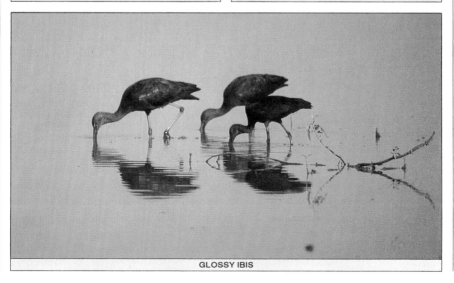

GLOSSY IBIS

DUCKS AND GEESE

By far the commonest duck seen in wetlands throughout Nigeria is the White-faced Tree-duck familiarly called the 'Wishi-Wishi' in imitation of its whistling call. The 'Wishi' is present all year round, unlike several species of Palearctic ducks which are dry season visitors only. This medium-sized duck stands more erect than most other ducks and is easily identified by the black head, white face, brown back and barred flanks. They are always found in flocks and feed by dabbling on marshy ground or open water, but will occasionally dive for food, which consists mainly of seeds and vegetable matter. Unlike most species of duck, the male and female are identical and both incubate the eggs, which are usually laid in a well-concealed nest on the ground. Within about 48 hours of hatching the ducklings are led to the water by the parents. Birds in immature plumage have pale grey faces rather than white, but sometimes the white faces of the adults become discoloured by dabbling in muddy places, and they can be mistaken for young birds.

The male Pigmy Goose is an attractive little bird which, in spite of the name, is actually classified as a duck rather than a goose. While the male has a distinctively patterned green and white head and reddish-brown body, the female is more drably coloured and lacks the green and white head. In flight the wings of both sexes are black with a conspicuous white wing-bar. Pigmy Geese are usually found in pairs or small groups and the favoured habitat is a lake or pond with waterlilies and weed, but as these ducks tend to dabble inconspicuously for food amongst the vegetation, they are often overlooked. In the water they are expert divers. The Pigmy Goose nests in a large hole in a hollow tree above water, sometimes as high as 20m and lays up to nine eggs.

In contrast to the tiny Pigmy Goose, the Spur-winged Goose is a large bird with a long neck, which gets its name from the sharp spur situated on the 'elbow' of its wing. Both sexes are mainly black above, glossed with green and white underneath with a white wing-patch which is revealed in flight. The beak and feet are pinkish red, and in the male the red extends to the front of the crown as the face is bare of feathers. The female Spur-wing is slightly smaller than the male. These geese are seen in flocks in marshes, wetlands and beside rivers and make their nests on the ground near water, laying up to nine eggs. They mainly feed by night on grasslands and farmlands and rest during the day. Spur-wings are widely distributed, but much more common in the wetlands from the great rivers northwards.

THE LILY-TROTTER AND THE BLACK CRAKE

These two waterbirds are both common residents in aquatic habitats throughout the country, but the Lily-trotter is much more likely to be seen, as it is not shy. The Lily-trotter is a long-legged, reddish-brown waterbird with a greyish shield on its forehead which turns blue in the breeding season. It is often seen picking its way delicately over waterlilies or other floating vegetation, supported by its extra-long toes, though it occasionally swims. In flight, the long legs trail untidily behind the bird, but it never flies far, and usually flies just above the surface of the water. Outside the breeding season Lily-trotters are gregarious and have a noisy, argumentative call. The nest is a floating platform of weed stems and only the male incubates the eggs. When the

WHITE-FACED TREE-DUCK

PYGMY GOOSE

SPUR-WINGED GOOSE

LILY-TROTTER

young first hatch, they are often carried by the male underneath his wings, the only visible sign being the small yellow legs dangling down beneath him. The immature bird lacks the frontal shield of the adult.

In contrast, the Black Crake is a secretive bird, usually glimpsed at the edge of reedbeds or rice paddies, creeping into the undergrowth to hide. It is a small glossy black waterbird with bright red legs and a yellow bill. It could be mistaken for a Moorhen, but the latter has white in its tail and white streaks on its flanks and greenish, not red, legs. This pair of crakes were photographed beside the rice paddies at IITA.

SENEGAL THICK-KNEE

The Senegal Thick-knee is found in pairs or small parties from the coast to the savanna, but only in suitable habitat near water, especially along sandy rivers. It feeds mainly at night, hence its large yellow eyes which help its night vision. When the bird is at rest during the day, its sandy-coloured plumage provides excellent camouflage. If it is disturbed it usually runs along the ground before taking flight. However, once in the air, the prominent white wing-bar is revealed and the bird becomes much more obvious. This photograph was taken at IITA where a small flock of Senegal Thick-knees live on the west bank of the lake. The nest is usually a shallow scrape on bare ground and both parents take care of the young. If danger threatens, the young bird will 'freeze' with head and neck outstretched on the ground so that it will not be spotted by a predator.

BLACK CRAKE

SENEGAL THICK-KNEE

WADERS

The Common Sandpiper is a familiar dry-season visitor to Nigeria, although a few non-breeding birds sometimes remain behind in the wet season when the majority have returned to Europe to breed. Small flocks of this little wader are frequently seen in waterside habitats from the coastal lagoons to the wetlands of the north. The Common Sandpiper is dark olive-brown above and white below, with faint streaks on its breast, but the best fieldmark is the white wing-bar noticeable in flight. It flies low over water with fluttering wing beats and short glides, uttering its piping 'tee wee wee' call. On land it constantly bobs its head and tail.

The Wood Sandpiper can be distinguished from the above bird by its white-spotted upperparts, its greyer breast, white rump, more prominent white eye-stripe and the lack of a white wing-bar when the bird is in flight. However, it also bobs its tail on landing. It is found in similar habitats to the Common Sandpiper but in smaller numbers. It too, is a dry season, non-breeding visitor to Nigeria. Both Sandpipers were photographed at IITA where large numbers are present in the dry season.

One of the most attractively patterned waders is the Painted Snipe. It is unusual because it is the female that is larger and has the more colourful plumage, as we have seen in Chapter Two. Their 'cryptic' plumage camouflages these birds so well that they blend into their surroundings and are difficult for predators to spot, especially since they 'freeze' and remain motionless for several minutes when disturbed. The female has a reddish brown head and chest with white round the eye whilst the male is mainly greyish brown, patterned with buff. The long bill of both sexes has a slight downward curve at the tip. It is the male which incubates the eggs and looks after the

COMMON SANDPIPER

PAINTED SNIPE

WOOD SANDPIPER

young, because after the last egg is laid, the female seeks another mate. The plumage of the immature bird resembles that of the male. The pair of Painted Snipe were photographed at IITA, feeding unobtrusively in the rice paddies.

PRATINCOLES

The Pratincole is a resident bird, found on muddy lake and river shores, and is often difficult to spot on the ground, because of its earth-coloured plumage. The only distinguishing mark is the pale throat bordered with black. In flight, the long wings and forked tail, give it a tern-like appearance. Pratincoles can sometimes be seen in the marshes near Lagos at the end of the wet season, but as they are most active at dawn and dusk, they may be overlooked.

The smaller, delicately marked Grey Pratincole, with its bright red legs, usually frequents the sandbanks of the large rivers, where it can sometimes be spotted, running in short spurts across the sand. At rest, these pale grey and white birds with buff throats are difficult to see against the whitish sand, but in flight the black and white wings and slightly forked tail helps identification. When the rivers are in flood Grey Pratincoles may move to coastal areas or inland waters such as IITA where this bird was photographed. Pratincoles mostly feed by catching insects in flight. The nest is a simple scrape in the sand, within 100 m of the water.

PLOVERS OF THE WATERSIDE

Plovers are small to medium-sized ground birds and several species of them are found near water, where they forage for food on the ground or in the mud at the water's edge. They are often distinctively marked, and are some of the most attractive birds to watch. Plovers nest on the ground and produce downy young which are able to run about within minutes of hatching. Most plovers practice distraction displays if their young are in danger by acting as if they are injured in order to draw any predator away from their chicks. They are strong fliers but can also run swiftly.

The Spur-winged Plover gets its name from the small spur on the 'elbow' joint of the wing, which can really only be seen if the bird is held in the hand. It is a common resident in small flocks along lake and river shores, mainly north of the great rivers, but there is a thriving population at IITA where they are relatively tame. When approached too closely they will usually run a little way and then bob up and down before taking wing and circling overhead, calling noisily. In flight the white wing-bar is obvious in the mainly black wing. The sexes are similar and in the breeding season, generally March to May, they are fearlessly aggressive if an intruder enters their territory, often making mock attacks accompanied by a persistent 'tic tic tic' call.

The White-headed Plover is perhaps the most beautiful of the West African plovers, with its black, grey, buff and white plumage and large yellow eye-wattles. In flight its wings are mainly white with black tips. It is not uncommon in small flocks on sandy riverbanks. It is subject to seasonal migrations, being more common in the south in the dry season but from June to October when the rivers are flooded and the sand-banks covered, it moves northwards as far as Sokoto and Yankari. It breeds during the dry season when the sandbanks are well above high-water level, and the

PRATINCOLE

GREY PRATINCOLE

WHITE-HEADED PLOVER

nest is a shallow scrape in sand or shingle. There is a small population at IITA where this photograph was taken, usually on the west bank of the lake.

One of the smallest plovers is the Kittlitz's Sand-plover. It is found on the margins of the great rivers, lakes and coastal lagoons, and although it is not seen in large numbers, it is widely distributed. It has dark upperparts, pale underparts with an rusty-buff wash and a white band round its forehead which continues round the back of its neck. It can be confused with the White-fronted Sand-plover but this bird does not have the black streak on the side of its face which is present on the Kittlitz's Sand-plover. This photograph was taken in the Hadejia Wetlands.

Another small plover usually found near water is the Forbes's Banded Plover pictured here feeding in a rice paddy, but it also inhabits open places with bare ground such as airfields, playing fields or recently burnt grassland. It has two dark bands across its chest and a brown head with a prominent white streak from the eye to the nape of the neck. The red skin round the eye also helps identification.

KINGFISHERS

The three kingfishers most likely to be seen in Nigerian wetlands are the Giant, the Pied and the tiny Malachite. Of these three the Pied Kingfisher is easily the most conspicuous because of its habit of hovering over a likely stretch of water before diving in to catch a fish. It will then return to a perch and knock the fish hard against the branch before swallowing it head-first. This male Pied Kingfisher was photographed

KITTLITZ'S SAND-PLOVER

FORBES'S BANDED PLOVER

on the Lekki Peninsula, just as it was about to enter its nest-burrow in a riverbank with food for its young. The fish is presented head-first to the nestlings so the fins do not catch in their throats. The female is similar to the male but has one incomplete chest band, instead of two. Pied Kingfishers nest in small colonies and are noisy birds, frequently making a loud twittering call, especially when disturbed at the nest site.

At about 45 cm long and with a massive black bill, the Giant Kingfisher is the largest African kingfisher. Although widely distributed, it is not common. Both sexes have a shaggy crest but the male has a rufous-coloured breast and black and white barred belly, whereas the female has the reverse: a blackish breast and rufous belly. The call is a loud rattling 'kek kek kek kek kek'. It is never found far from water and prefers tree-lined banks. As it usually fishes from a concealed perch, it is difficult to spot, and often the first sight of a Giant Kingfisher is of a large black and rufous bird flying off low across the water, calling loudly. They are solitary nesters and dig an earth burrow in a riverbank or cliff.

In contrast, the tiny crested Malachite Kingfisher is only 14 cm from the tip of its bright red bill to the end of its tail. It is found from the coastal mangrove swamps to the extreme north of the country wherever there are lakes, streams or marshes. With its brilliant purplish-blue, rufous and white plumage, it resembles a living jewel as it darts from its perch overlooking the water to catch a fish. It can be confused with the slightly smaller Pigmy Kingfisher but the latter has no crest and is usually found away from water. A solitary nester, the Malachite Kingfisher constructs an earth burrow in a bank or earth mound. The immature bird has a black bill for its first three months.

PIED KINGFISHER

GIANT KINGFISHER

MALACHITE KINGFISHER

Chapter Six

BIRDS OF THE FOREST ZONE

This area includes the forest, derived savanna and mangrove swamps of the south of the country. True forest birds are notoriously difficult to see as they live either high up in the canopy of the forest or in the shady undergrowth, but nevertheless there is something magical about walking in a forest like Okomu in the early morning, listening to the bird-song and catching a brief glimpse of large forest hornbills or Giant Blue Plantain-eaters flying from tree to tree. Within the forest itself, birds are more often heard than seen, so it is important to learn their calls in order to identify them. The south of Nigeria has extensive waterside habitats, so many of the water birds covered in the previous chapter are found in this part of the country too, making it a rewarding area for the keen birdwatcher.

BIRDS OF PREY

The Palm-nut Vulture sometimes known as the Vulturine Fish Eagle, is unique amongst vultures as it is mainly vegetarian. It is chiefly found where there are oil-palms, as the outside flesh of the palm-nut is its main food. It is common in the south of the country and is frequently seen on the Lekki Peninsula, especially in the coastal creeks, where it scavenges on dead fish, crabs and scraps. This large black and white vulture with broad wings is an impressive sight as it soars overhead. The adult has a red face and large hooked beak but the immature bird has a yellowish face and is a dull mottled brown. Palm-nut Vultures build large stick nests in tall trees, often using the same nest for several years.

The Harrier Hawk is a peculiar long-legged, grey hawk which is common in the forest zone but less so further north because, like the Palm-nut Vulture, one of its main sources of food is the flesh of palm-nuts. It has broad wings, a long black tail banded with white and from the lower breast downwards is barred black and white. However, this hawk has two most unusual features: firstly the long 'double-jointed' legs which can bend at an angle of 70° to enable it to extract prey from holes in trees or in the ground, and secondly the bare yellow face which flushes red with excitement when catching prey or during courtship. It is a strange sight to see this large bird clinging to a treetrunk, branch or even a riverbank, while it investigates a hole for prey, flapping its wings from time to time to maintain its balance.

BLACK-AND-WHITE-TAILED HORNBILL

Another familiar bird on the Lekki Peninsula is the Black-and-white-tailed (or Allied) Hornbill which can often be seen in small flocks flying across the road with its weak,

PALM-NUT VULTURE

JUVENILE HARRIER HAWK

undulating 'flap flap glide' style of flight. This medium-sized black and white hornbill with its broad, pale yellow bill lined with black, can be confused with the black and white Piping Hornbill but the latter bird has more white on its wings and a darker bill. The Black-and-white-tailed Hornbill often calls excitedly from the treetops, making a loud, shrill 'pi,pi,pi - pi,pi,pi' call as it stretches its neck up and rocks backwards and forwards. Like other hornbills, this Hornbill nests in a hole in a tree and the nest-hole is walled up with mud, leaving only a small opening through which to feed the female and young, as described in Chapter Two.

BROAD-BILLED ROLLER

The Broad-billed Roller is another noisy bird found in the forest zone. It is present in the dry season, but most birds migrate to the savanna areas during the rains. This is the smallest and least colourful of the rollers found in Nigeria, but it is conspicuous because of its habit of perching on the tops of trees uttering harsh nasal cries and aggressively attacking intruders. The Broad-billed Roller will even 'see-off' much larger birds such as the Harrier Hawk if it strays into its territory. This chunky bird is cinnamon brown in colour with purplish blue underparts becoming azure-blue under the tail and a conspicuous yellow bill. As this roller catches insects on the wing, it has the long swept-back wings of an expert flyer, like a falcon. It drinks by skimming low over water, dipping in its beak like a swallow. Like other rollers, the Broad-billed nests in holes high up in a tree.

BLUE-BREASTED KINGFISHER

The Blue-breasted Kingfisher can be confused with the much more common Senegal Kingfisher, but is larger, has a blue, not grey breast and has more black on the wings. Both kingfishers have red upper mandibles and black lower mandibles. The Blue-breasted Kingfisher is commoner in the forest zone although its range extends into the wooded savanna. This kingfisher is found mostly along rivers and wooded estuaries, although mainly insectivorous, but it also feeds on crabs in mangrove swamps which is one of its favourite habitats. It is shyer than the Senegal Kingfisher and much less frequently seen but because of its similarity it can be over-looked unless the call, a whistling 'piou-piou-piou', is known.

BEE-EATERS

The White-throated Bee-eater is also only present in the forest zone in the dry season when, for example, it is common in the derived savanna close to Lagos. Flocks frequent the area behind Lighthouse beach and are also seen on the Lekki Peninsula. This elegant greenish-blue bird has a white throat clearly marked with a black chestband, a black stripe through the eye and a black crown. The adult has two long tail streamers which give it a swallow-like appearance in flight as it hawks for insects. Like other bee-eaters, it will return to a perch to knock out the sting before eating a bee. At the beginning of the rains White-throated Bee-eaters migrate to the extreme north of Nigeria and into Niger to breed. Flocks of them therefore pass through the

BLACK-AND-WHITE-TAILED HORNBILL

BROAD-BILLED ROLLER

BLUE-BREASTED KINGFISHER

WHITE-THROATED BEE-EATER

savanna areas twice a year, to and from their breeding grounds, keeping their flocks together by constant calling. These bee-eaters nest in loose colonies in burrows dug in banks or in flat ground, and lay up to seven white eggs. Unmated birds will help the parents feed the chicks, and there may be several nest-helpers or 'nannies' to one nest burrow.

The beautiful Rosy Bee-eaters, with their charcoal grey backs, broad white streak below the eye and rosy breasts, are widely dispersed in the rainforest and moist savanna areas when not breeding, in flocks of about 10-50. They spend much of the time on the wing, perching occasionally, but always high up on the tops of the tallest trees. They move north to their breeding grounds in April, at the beginning of the wet season and one of the most spectacular ornithological sights in Nigeria is to see a colony of many thousands of Rosy Bee-eaters gathering on the sandbanks of one of the great rivers to dig their nesting burrows.

GABON WOODPECKER

The Gabon Woodpecker is a small forest woodpecker with olive-green upperparts and heavily streaked yellowish underparts. The male (seen here excavating a nesting hole in a dead tree) has a scarlet crown whereas in the female this is dark brown. Its stiff tail helps support it while it is clinging to a tree, as it feeds mainly on grubs found in decaying wood. These woodpeckers are far from common, unlike the larger Grey Woodpecker which is a much more familiar bird, even nesting in gardens and compounds.

ROSY BEE-EATER

GABON WOODPECKER

Chapter Seven

BIRDS OF THE WOODLAND SAVANNA

The woodland (or Guinea) savanna includes most of the central area of Nigeria between the forest zone to the south and the dry grasslands to the north. As the two great rivers, the Niger and the Benue, flow mainly through this region, they provide an important habitat for many waterbirds too, like the Grey Pratincole, for example, which is described in the Chapter Five. Although several of the birds included in this chapter are present in other parts of the country, the woodland savanna is their main habitat and the following are some of the familiar birds of this area.

CATTLE EGRET

Of the many birds of the African savanna, perhaps the Cattle Egret is the bird which has most successfully adapted its habits to fit in with those of man. Once they used to follow the herds of wild game to feed on the insects disturbed as they grazed, now they mainly follow domestic cattle instead. This small white egret with its stubby

CATTLE EGRET

yellow bill and greenish legs is a great opportunist and will even perch in a tree in bloom, to eat the large numbers of insects attracted by the flowers. At night the egrets roost in trees, usually near water, and flocks flying in a V-formation are a common sight in the evenings. During the breeding season this egret acquires buff-coloured plumes on its head and neck. Because of its adaptability, the Cattle Egret is even found in Lagos, but its main habitat is the savanna because of the large herds of cattle.

BIRDS OF PREY

By far the commonest species of vulture in Nigeria is the Hooded Vulture which is found mainly around towns and villages in the savanna although patchily distributed in the south. The Hooded Vulture is a smallish, dark brown vulture with a short rounded tail. The pink face is bare, with greyish down on the back of its head and neck. In flight, like other vultures, it often glides with its wings splayed out like 'fingers', which smooths the air flow and helps to maintain its stability. In spite of their ugly appearance, vultures serve a very useful purpose as 'flying dustmen' by cleaning up the carcasses of dead animals and human rubbish, thus preventing the spread of disease. However, this vulture is becoming scarcer everywhere, as with fewer wild animals left and cleaner towns, there is less carrion on which to feed.

Although the Black Kite is the most frequently seen bird of prey in Nigeria, it is chiefly a savanna resident. During the rains it is absent from the south, although it does breed there in the dry season. In spite of its name, the Black Kite is a dark brown bird with a yellow bill, but in flight it is easily recognised by its forked tail. It also feeds mainly by scavenging and so, like the Hooded Vulture, is common around towns and villages. Both species will sometimes feed on animals killed by cars on the road, only flapping into the air at the last minute when a vehicle approaches. Black Kites will also congregate at the edges of a bush fire to catch the insects and small animals escaping from the flames. The nest is a bulky structure, built in a tall tree, and the young birds remain in the nest for about six weeks after hatching.

Of all the eagles of the African savanna, the strikingly handsome Bateleur is the most beautiful bird of prey. It is an acrobatic flier with a complete mastery of the air. Its black, white and reddish-brown plumage are enhanced by the bright red of its face and legs. In flight the Bateleur is unmistakable because of its long wings and short tail with legs protruding beyond it. The juvenile bird retains its brown plumage for several years and can be mistaken for another species. The Bateleur prefers the drier areas of the savanna but is seen at both Lake Kainji and the Yankari Game Reserve.

The strange looking Long-crested Hawk-eagle is mainly dark brown with a long untidy crest on its head which blows in the wind when it is perched on the top of a tree. It has white legs, and in flight it is easily identifiable by the large white patches on its wings. It mostly feeds on small rodents which it drops on swiftly from its perch. It swallows small prey items whole because of its large gape, but will tear up larger prey. Because it feeds on small mice and rats it is of particular benefit to farmers. This bird was photographed near the rice paddies just outside Bida, in Niger State.

The Red-tailed Buzzard is the largest buzzard in Nigeria with the typical broad wings of its kind. Although seen in the south in the dry season, it too is mainly a savanna resident where it can spot its prey more easily. The upperparts, throat and

HOODED VULTURE

BLACK KITE

BATALEUR

LONG-CRESTED HAWK-EAGLE

RED-TAILED BUZZARD

chest are mainly brown with the underparts white, spotted with brown. The reddish brown tail is obvious when the bird is in flight or perched. The young buzzard does not have the dark chest of the adult.

The Grasshopper Buzzard is smaller, and feeds mainly on grasshoppers and locusts. These buzzards are often seen perching on trees beside the road scouting for insects, but are more easily recognised in flight by the reddish-brown wing-patch. The upperparts are darkish brown, the breast buff-coloured with dark streaks. It too, is attracted to bush fires, to feed on the escaping insects.

The Black-shouldered Kite is one of the few birds of prey which, like the Kestrel, hovers in the air when searching for prey on the ground. This smallish grey and white bird with the distinctive black shoulder patches is a graceful flyer, and is more common in the savanna where prey is easier to spot, although it is also present in small numbers in the derived savanna of the south. It feeds mainly on small rodents so is useful to farmers. The immature bird has brownish plumage with the underparts streaked with yellowish brown.

The Fox Kestrel is almost entirely restricted to inselbergs, the huge bare rocks which dot the savannas of Nigeria, so these birds are not commonly seen. Both male and female are reddish-brown, streaked with black and have a long tail barred with black. These kestrels nest in inaccessible holes and ledges in the rock, and use the same site year after year. This bird was photographed near Wase Rock in Plateau State.

The large Spotted Eagle-owl is relatively common in the savanna where its preferred habitat is near towns and villages, but being nocturnal, it is not often seen by day. The plumage is greyish, finely marked with brown and white, and it has distinctive ear-tufts. Because the Spotted Eagle-owl feeds largely on mice and rats which destroy much of the farmer's grain, it should be welcomed for its pest-control activities rather than feared.

GRASSHOPPER BUZZARD

BLACK-SHOULDERED KITE

FOX KESTREL

ROLLERS

The Abyssinian Roller is one of the most beautiful of the birds of the African 'bush' with its azure-blue, purple and brown plumage and graceful tail streamers. Fortunately for the birdwatcher, it perches conspicuously on telegraph wires or trees to watch for its insect prey, so it is easily spotted on road journeys in the central and northern areas of Nigeria. However, it is subject to local migrations. During the breeding season between March and June, the birds become noisy and pugnacious and give spectacular displays of 'stooping' and rolling flight, calling raucously to chase away intruders. The nest is in a hole in a tree or similar cavity, and like most hole-nesters, the eggs are white. A few European Rollers visit Nigeria during the dry season and are very similar but can be distinguished by the square tail rather than the long tail streamers of the Abyssinian Roller.

The handsome Blue-bellied Roller is a slightly smaller bird, but more thickset than the Abyssinian. It is less common and only locally distributed in the savanna, mainly in the north-west where the author has most frequently encountered it in Niger State and Abuja. The head and breast are a pale pinkish fawn, the back black, the belly a rich purplish-blue and the light-blue tail deeply forked. In the breeding season these birds are very noisy and utter a loud 'ah-ah-ah-ah' on the wing or call from treetops. Like other rollers, they nest in tree-holes, and lay white eggs.

VINACEOUS DOVE

One of the most familiar sounds of the Nigerian savanna is the monotonous 'coo-coo coo coo' of the Vinaceous Dove whose call can best be remembered by the phrase 'Better go home! Better go home!' This small, pale greyish dove has a black collar on its hind neck. When the bird alights on a tree it utters a sharp nasal call and fans its

ABYSSINIAN ROLLER

SPOTTED EAGLE-OWL

BLUE-BELLIED ROLLER

tail so that the white tips and black band are clearly seen. Like most other doves, it builds a flimsy stick nest in a tree and lays two oval white eggs. The bird in this picture was dozing in the heat of the day.

SENEGAL WATTLED PLOVER

Probably the commonest plover of the woodland savanna, the Senegal Wattled Plover is a long-legged plover with pale brown plumage which camouflages it well on the ground. In flight however, the black and white on the wings make it easily visible. Its white crown is bordered with black and the throat streaked, but the most distinctive feature is the long yellow wattle on either side of the bill. Although this plover is often found near water, it is also found in grassy areas far from water. In the breeding season the Senegal Wattled Plover is a noisy, demonstrative bird which mobs intruders into its territory with sharp cries of 'yip yip yip'. The immature bird lacks the yellow wattles of the adult.

LONG-TAILED SHRIKE

The Long-tailed Shrike is a noisy bird usually seen in small parties, flying short distances from tree to tree, one after the other. Its plumage is streaky-brown above and buff below but the most distinctive feature is the long tail which is constantly

VINACEOUS DOVE

SENEGAL WATTLED PLOVER

LONG-TAILED SHRIKE

jerked up and down or waved in a characteristic circular movement. In flight the reddish brown wing-patch can be seen. The hooked beak is bright yellow. These shrikes feed mainly on the ground, where they move with long hops as they search for insects and small lizards. Long-tailed Shrikes are common in savanna areas and often seen in gardens. They build large cup-shaped nests in the fork of a tree and lay 3-4 eggs.

BEE-EATERS

The attractive Red-throated Bee-eater is a common resident locally in the northern woodland savanna (although present in smaller numbers in the southern savanna) especially where there are high-banked streams and erosion gullies suitable for nesting colonies. This bee-eater is usually found in small parties and can be distinguished by the bright red throat, green upperparts, buff breast, the black band through the eye and the long curved bill. Bees and other insects are caught on the wing, mostly at treetop level, and then beaten against a branch to remove the venom before they are swallowed. Its graceful, gliding flight and twittering call is characteristic. Red-throated Bee-eaters nest in the dry season in closely grouped earth burrows in colonies of between 5-150 pairs.

Another brightly coloured bee-eater is the Carmine Bee-eater. It is carmine-red all over except for the greenish-blue head and pale blue rump and has long projecting tail

RED-THROATED BEE-EATER

CARMINE BEE-EATER

feathers. This is a bird of the open savanna but is commonly seen in the rice paddies near Bida and usually breeds in huge colonies in river banks (see Chapter Two). These bee-eaters are attracted to bush fires to feast on the insects escaping the flames and will also perch on the backs of cattle or other animals to catch the insects disturbed as the animals walk through the grass. These beautiful birds are a great asset to farmers as they catch huge numbers of destructive insects, and should be protected at all costs.

The smallest bee-eater found in Nigeria is the Little Bee-eater which is a handsome green bird with a bright yellow throat and blackish chestband. It is not uncommon throughout the country, from the Lekki Peninsula in the south to Nguru in the north, but is more frequently seen in the savanna zone. These bee-eaters favour waterside areas with tall grasses such as marshes and floodplains, where they are usually seen in pairs or family groups hawking flying insects from a perch on a tall grass stem or low bush, often only about a metre from the ground. Little Bee-eaters are solitary nesters and breed towards the beginning of the wet season, digging an earth burrow in a river bank or similar site. The immature bird does not have a black chestband and the throat is buff rather than yellow.

YELLOW-THROATED LONG-CLAW

Seen from behind, the Yellow-throated Long-claw appears to be a typical dull, brown-streaked pipit but when seen from the front the brilliant yellow underparts with the black 'gorget' marking its throat, transform it into a most striking bird. These birds, which are always seen in pairs, get their name from the unusually long hind claw. They have a characteristic fluttering and gliding flight, which reveals the white in their tails. Although these birds are seen in grassy areas throughout Nigeria, they are most common in the savanna and spend much of the time feeding on the ground. They breed in the rains, building their nests in grassy tufts.

LITTLE BEE-EATER

YELLOW-THROATED LONG-CLAW

Chapter Eight

BIRDS OF THE DRY SAVANNA

This region covers the far north of Nigeria where the dry season lasts for many months, the rains are brief and vegetation grows progressively sparser towards the border with Niger. Some of the birds in this area are found in other parts of Nigeria but have been included in this chapter as this is their main area of occurrence. This region also contains the Hadejia Wetlands, so many of the waterbirds described in Chapter Five, like storks, waders and ducks are found in this extensive wetland area too. Birds are easy to see in this open landscape and travellers cannot fail to see flocks of slender Long-tailed Doves perched on the thorn-bushes beside the road, or catch glimpses of Red-beaked Hornbills 'tooting' from the tops of trees, but the following are some of the other common birds of the dry savanna.

BIRDS OF PREY

The White-backed Vulture is larger and much less common than the Hooded Vulture. Although it prefers the drier savanna, it is found as far south as the Yankari Game Reserve in the dry season, which is just within the woodland savanna area. Mainly pale brown with a bare black head and a white ruff at the base of the neck, the white back is only visible in flight, as it is covered by the wings when the bird is at rest. The long neck and beak are particularly adapted to eating the soft flesh and internal

WHITE-BACKED VULTURE

organs of a carcass. Like most vultures, White-backed Vultures will gorge themselves on a dead animal until they can hardly fly, and will then rest on the ground with out-stretched wings. The one pictured here is by its nest in a borassus palm in the Reserve.

The Nubian, or Lappet-faced Vulture, is one of the largest African vultures and has a massive hooked beak adapted to eating the skin and bones which White-backed Vultures leave, so these two species of vulture can live together without competing for the same food source. The plumage is mainly brown with thick, white down underneath and the skin of the neck and head is pink. This vulture too, prefers an arid climate and is uncommon in Nigeria, but is also occasionally seen at Yankari, where this photograph was taken.

The Dark Chanting Goshawk, a long-legged, mainly grey bird of prey, is fairly common in northern Nigeria. These birds can often be seen perched on telegraph posts or trees, with their characteristic upright stance, watching intently for prey on the ground below. The upperparts and throat are grey, with the belly and thighs finely barred with black and white. The cere, the base of its beak and the legs are orangey-red. The Chanting Goshawk feeds mainly on lizards, small snakes, small mammals and insects, which it mostly catches on the ground. It gets its name from the 'chanting' cry that the male utters repeatedly during the breeding season. The stick nest, sometimes lined with mud or grass, is built in a thorny tree by both sexes and the female lays 1-2 eggs. If two eggs are laid, usually only the first chick to hatch survives. The immature bird differs from the adult as it is brownish, with a streaked throat and is barred brown and white instead of grey and white like the adult.

Two birds of prey which are very similar to each other, are the Pallid Harrier and Montagu's Harrier, both of which are only seen in the dry season as they are migrants from Europe which winter mainly in the wetlands of the north. The males of these two species are both pale grey with black wing-tips and white rumps but can be distinguished by the fact that the Montagu's Harrier has a black bar on the upper wing and reddish-brown markings on the underwing, which the Pallid Harrier does not. However, although the females of both species are very different from their males, as they are brown, not grey, with white rumps, they are almost identical to each other and it is practically impossible to tell them apart in the field. The female in the photograph seen near Dagona Lake, is almost certainly a Pallid Harrier because of the darker circle of feathers below the white eye-patch. These harriers behave in a very different way from the Chanting Goshawk, as they spend much of the day on the wing, quartering marshes for small mammals and insects by flying a few feet above the ground. They spend little time perching and roost at night in groups on the ground. Like other Palearctic migrants, they do not breed in Nigeria.

SPECKLED PIGEON

Although the range of the Speckled Pigeon extends as far south as Ibadan and even to Lagos, it is most common in the dry savanna, especially on farmland around towns and villages where there is a plentiful supply of grain. This large, well-built pigeon appears pale grey at a distance, but at close quarters the beautifully patterned purplish brown and white speckles on its back can be seen. The most distinctive fieldmark is the patch of bright-red skin around the eye. Speckled Pigeons often feed in flocks on

NUBIAN VULTURE

DARK CHANTING GOSHAWK

PALLID HARRIER

the ground in the morning and evening, but mostly shelter in trees in the hottest part of the day. Here, they are perched on a dum palm beside Dagona Lake near Nguru.

BLUE-EARED GLOSSY STARLING

One of the most handsomely coloured birds of the dry savanna is the Blue-eared Glossy Starling with its metallic glossy, greenish-blue back, purple belly and conspicuous yellow eye. It gets its name from the bright blue feathers covering its ears (ear-coverts). It is common wherever there are Neem trees, especially around Sokoto and Maiduguri. However, several species of starling are very similar and it is not easy to tell them apart, but the Purple Glossy Starling for example, is more common in the woodland savanna. All starlings are noisy birds and the Blue-eared Glossy Starling has a variety of shrill, whistling calls. These birds are usually seen in flocks feeding on the ground or in Neem trees, on the fleshy fruit. They nest in tree-holes, lining the hole with grass and feathers, and lay three or four pale greenish-blue eggs.

FOUR-BANDED SANDGROUSE

The Four-banded Sandgrouse, although mainly a bird of the dry sandy savanna, may be found as far south as the Lake Kainji Reserve in the dry season, however. The male, pictured here, has a black and white forehead and bands of reddish-brown, white and black across its chest. The female has similar colouring but lacks the distinctive bands on forehead and chest. These birds are usually seen in small flocks, but as their

SPECKLED PIGEON

BLUE-EARED GLOSSY STARLING

colouring camouflages them so well, they are often not spotted until they fly off, when the black wing-tips are visible. Like many ground-nesting birds, the nest is a simple depression in the ground. The chicks are covered with down and able to leave the nest soon after hatching.

CRESTED LARK

The sandy-coloured Crested Lark is more common in the drier north of the country. A sturdy lark with a largish crest and dark streaks on its breast, it prefers grassy areas and farmland and is most often seen on the ground. The song is a pleasant fluty sound, which it usually sings from the ground rather than in flight. Crested larks construct a nest from grass and feathers in a hollow on the ground and lay 2-4 buff coloured eggs, heavily speckled with purplish-brown.

WHEATEAR

Another bird which is mainly seen on the ground is the Wheatear but unlike the Crested Lark, this bird is a Palearctic migrant, so is only present in the dry season when wearing its less conspicuous, non-breeding plumage. The most distinctive feature is the white rump which is clearly visible in flight. Otherwise the bird is mainly buff with black wings and a white eye-stripe. The Wheatear is a restless bird, which frequently bobs and 'flirts' its tail, and often perches on low stumps, or termite mounds.

FOUR-BANDED SANDGROUSE

CRESTED LARK

WHEATEAR

ANT-CHAT   BUSH-SPARROW

ANT-CHAT

The Ant-chat is a plain, blackish bird mostly seen in small flocks feeding on the ground. Close to, however, the light coloured edges to the sooty-brown feathers give it a slightly dappled appearance as can be seen in the picture. In flight the large white wing-patches are obvious. However, at a distance the Ant-chat can be confused with the Chestnut-bellied Starling which also has light patches on its wings in flight, although at close quarters the starling is seen to be completely different, with a reddish-brown belly and a white eye.

BUSH-SPARROW

This pair of Bush-sparrows are at their nesting hole in an old dum palm. These dull-looking brown and grey birds are usually seen in small parties feeding on seeds on the ground, although they sometimes search for insects in the trees. They are not uncommon, although subject to some seasonal movements, but because of their unobtrusive colouring they may not always be noticed. Their frequent noisy chirping is characteristic of the sparrow family. The nest, in a hole in a tree or even a fallen log on the ground, is lined with feathers, fur and grass.

Chapter Nine

BIRDWATCHING AS A HOBBY IN NIGERIA

If the previous chapters have caught your imagination, by now you will most probably want to know how to begin birdwatching so that you can experience the fascination of studying Nigerian birds for yourself. To get the most enjoyment out of this hobby, however, there are a number of things to consider such as WHEN? WHERE? and HOW?

When?

In the tropics the night is nearly 12 hours long and as most birds are unable to feed in the dark, by the morning they are extremely hungry. When they are breeding they also need to re-establish their territories by singing at the start of a new day. This chorus of birdsong together with the more intense feeding activity, makes morning the best time to watch birds. The keen birdwatcher has to be 'up with the lark' as the saying goes, as it is true that 'the early bird catches the worm!' Luckily, of course, the early mornings are the coolest and most pleasant time of day for the birdwatcher in Nigeria's hot climate. Activity generally declines in the middle of the day as birds shelter from the heat, but about four o'clock in the afternoon there is another spurt of activity. This continues until dark as the birds search for their last meal of the day. Some birds like Cattle Egrets collect together to roost on a particular tree. If you know of a roosting place it is interesting to watch the egrets congregating on the branches in the evening, looking like candles on a Christmas tree, but never get too close, or you will disturb them.

During the breeding season, which varies from one species to the next, birds are more obvious because they are busy nest-building and feeding their young. Woodpeckers, starlings and barbets, for example, are often busy round their tree nestholes in the dry season. If you are lucky enough to spot a bird going in or out of a hole, watch quietly from a concealed position. If there are young in the nest, the parent birds will make frequent visits carrying food in their bills. However, be careful never to disturb them as the birds may desert the nest, abandoning the eggs to grow cold or the nestlings to starve to death.

Palearctic migrants are present in Nigeria during the dry season, so this is the best time of year to look for waders along the coast or by inland marshes and wetlands. Remember though, if you are watching birds in a tidal estuary, the waders will only come in to feed when the mud flats are exposed at low tide. At high tide the mud will be covered with water and only seabirds like terns and cormorants can feed, or possibly herons and egrets if the water is shallow enough.

Another advantage to the birdwatcher in the dry season is that the savanna trees have fewer leaves so the birds are easier to spot. The bush tracks are also firmer for both vehicles and walkers if you are bird-watching in the 'bush'. However, in the wet season the male weavers, bishops and wydahs are in their colourful breeding plumage and are much more conspicuous, so at any time of year there are interesting birds to see, if you know when and where to look.

Where?

Because many birds live on or near water, and all birds need to drink, a lake, river or marsh is always a good place to watch birds. Wherever there are trees too, you will find birds, and especially in compounds where there are flowering plants, or shrubs and trees with berries. Even in cities Kestrels have colonised tower blocks as these provide nesting places which resemble the cliff ledges that are their natural habitat. Swifts too have adapted to city-life, and both these species can be spotted in the skies above Lagos. However, there are many places in Nigeria which are especially good for bird-watchers, like the Game Reserves and the Hadejia Wetlands. These are listed at the end of the chapter

How?

A pair of binoculars is a great advantage to the birdwatcher, but not essential. Young people mostly have excellent eyesight. However, if you do want to buy binoculars, the preferred sizes for birdwatchers are 8 x 40 or 10 x 40. They should be properly focused and aligned, and always kept clean.

To set a pair of binoculars for your own eyes:

1. Look at the binoculars and find the focusing wheel and the adjusting eyepiece.
2. Using your hand or one of the lens caps, cover the right-hand lens.
3. Focus the left eye using the focusing wheel.
4. Remove the hand or lens cap and place over the left-hand lens.
5. Focus the right eye using the adjusting eyepiece and note the correct setting.
6. Remove the lens cap from the left-hand lens.
7. Before going birdwatching, check the adjusting eye-piece is on the correct setting, and then only use the focusing wheel to obtain perfect focus.

When going birdwatching it is better to wear dull-coloured clothes which blend in with the surroundings. Walk slowly and quietly, without making sudden movements that will scare the birds away. Always try to walk with the sun behind you so that it shines on the bird and lights up its plumage. If you look towards the sun you will only see a frustrating silhouette and the colours will be indiscernible. Watch for any movement around you, as it is usually the movement of a bird which alerts the eye to its presence, but also keep your ears alert to listen for birdcalls or songs.

If you want to get closer to a bird, do not walk directly towards it, but approach it obliquely, as this will be less likely to alarm it. Cars can be very useful mobile hides, and if, for example, you should see a marsh beside the road with interesting birds, it is often better to park the car off the road and remain inside, as by getting out you could frighten the birds away. In Europe bird-watchers sometimes purchase expensive canvas 'hides' with window openings cut in them so that they can watch birds without being seen. In Nigeria though, suitable materials literally grow on trees! Palm fronds or matting can quickly be made into an excellent hide.

What is it?

When you see a bird you do not know, you will want to identify it, so it is best to take a notebook and pencil with you for field observations. Study the bird carefully and look for its distinctive features:

What size is it?
What colour is its plumage?
What colour is its bill, and how long is it?
How long are its legs, and what colour are they?
Does it have a stripe over its eye?
Does it have a bar of lighter coloured feathers on its wing?
How long is its tail and does it have any distinctive stripes or spots?
How is it behaving?
What call or song is it making?
What is the habitat? i.e. wetland, forest, grassland etc.

When you have made a mental note of all these features, make a written note of relevant points in your notebook, a quick sketch if possible, and only then try to identify the bird from the field guide. Sometimes a bird flies off quickly, so do not waste time searching in the field guide immediately – concentrate on making a thorough observation of the bird before it is too late. When making an identification, remember that some birds have different plumage patterns between males and females, adults and juveniles, and between their breeding and non-breeding plumage. Also, some distinctive markings can only be seen in flight.

The Squacco Heron is a good example of this. In flight the bird looks like a white egret with a barely noticeable strip of buff-coloured feathers along its back. When the bird alights and folds its wings, the white disappears instantly and the whole appearance is of a brownish bird so well camouflaged that it seems to have disappeared from view. The wing-bars on the Common Sandpiper and the Black-tailed Godwit are also only visible in flight, so keep an eye on the bird as it flies away. The patterns on the wings of plovers are often very distinctive, like the White-headed Plover. When its wings are closed they are mainly black, but when they are open they are almost entirely white. The white rumps on some birds are only visible in flight too, when the wings are open, like the often solitary Green Sandpiper.

Some Good Birdwatching Areas in Nigeria

1. The Lekki Peninsula near Lagos: remnants of forest, derived savanna, marshes and mangrove swamps.
2. The International Institute for Tropical Agriculture, Ibadan (IITA): forest, farmland, rice paddies, lake and marshes. This Institute, however, can only be visited with prior permission.
3. Okomu Forest Reserve, in Edo State near Udo: rainforest, oil-palm plantations and a riverine area.
4. Oban and Okwango sections of the Cross River National Park: primary rainforest.
5. Obudu Cattle Ranch, Obudu Plateau: montane forest and grasslands.
6. Mambilla Plateau; montane forest and grasslands, with the Gashaka-Gumti National Park near Serti, Taraba State.

7. Lake Kainji National Park, Borgu Sector, Kwara State: Guinea savanna, with the Oli River running through the park; Zurgurma Sector, Niger State.

8. Pandam Wildlife Reserve, Plateau State, between Lafia and Shendam: Guinea savanna and a lake.

9. Wase Rock, near Langtang in Plateau State; a volcanic plug surrounded by Guinea savanna.

10. Kamuku Game Reserve, Birnin Gwari, Kaduna State, Guinea savanna.

11. Kagoro Forest Reserve, Kaduna State: a pocket of moist forest in the savanna area.

12. Yankari Game Reserve, Bauchi State: Guinea savanna, with the Gaji river running through the reserve, and marshes beside the river.

13. Sambisa Game Reserve in Borno State: Sudan savanna.

14. Hadejia-Nguru Wetlands in Jigawa, Yobe and Bauchi States: extensive wetlands, including Dagona Wildfowl Reserve near Nguru. Sudan savanna and arid thornscrub.

15. Lake Chad area, Borno State, Sudan savanna and marshes.

These are the major bird-watching areas in Nigeria, and information about how to get to these areas and suitable accommodation nearby can be found in 'Enjoy Nigeria' by Ian Nason, published by Spectrum Books of Ibadan in 1991. However, there are birds to be seen practically everywhere. Although there may not be a great variety of species where you live, there are likely to be plenty of interesting birds to watch. Go outside, LOOK and LISTEN then make a note of what you have seen. Bird-watching can become an absorbing hobby which can last a lifetime.

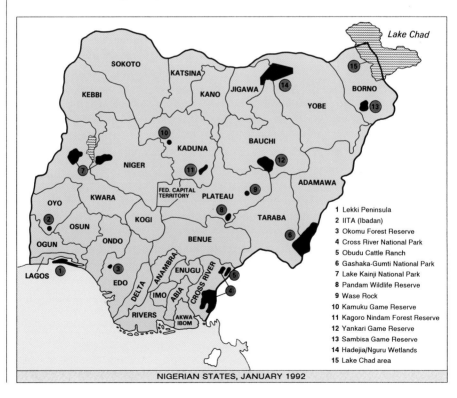

1	Lekki Peninsula
2	IITA (Ibadan)
3	Okomu Forest Reserve
4	Cross River National Park
5	Obudu Cattle Ranch
6	Gashaka-Gumti National Park
7	Lake Kainji National Park
8	Pandam Wildlife Reserve
9	Wase Rock
10	Kamuku Game Reserve
11	Kagoro Nindam Forest Reserve
12	Yankari Game Reserve
13	Sambisa Game Reserve
14	Hadejia/Nguru Wetlands
15	Lake Chad area

NIGERIAN STATES, JANUARY 1992

Chapter Ten

THE IMPORTANCE OF CONSERVATION IN NIGERIA

Nature conservation is one of the most important issues in the world today as the whole future of mankind on Planet Earth depends upon the way we look after our environment. We have already seen in the introduction how dependent every living creature is upon each other, and how our future is closely related to the fate of birds and animals and their habitat. Now it is time to study this interdependence in more detail. Nature conservation must become an integral part of our efforts to resolve the world's problems – human, environmental and economic. This can best be illustrated by using the example of the drought-stricken areas of Africa.

Drought occurs when the rains fail, and crops wither and die. When this happens, the people in their desperation begin to cut down the remaining trees and shrubs, not only for firewood but also to feed their animals. The result is that before long all ground cover is removed and the soil is exposed to wind erosion which destroys the fertility of the land. To prevent the land turning into a desert, trees must be replanted and protected from livestock until they form a barrier to stop the advancing sand-dunes. Only when they are mature can they be used again in a sustainable way. However, it is vital to involve the people who live in the area in any such scheme and to explain to them what is being done for their benefit. It can only be successfully achieved with their co-operation, otherwise they will resent the project as a threat to their livelihood.

In the tropical regions of the world the importance of saving the rainforest cannot be over-estimated, as it has a beneficial effect on the climate of the entire planet. The tropical rainforests are literally the 'lungs of the earth', as they absorb enormous quantities of carbon-dioxide (which is the gas mainly responsible for global warming) and release the oxygen we need in order to breathe, into the atmosphere. Although the serious consequences of global warming on our climate are well known, it seems that little is being done about preventing further destruction of the rainforest. An excess of carbon-dioxide in the atmosphere could result in the climate of the earth heating up and the ice-caps beginning to melt. This in turn would cause the sea level to rise and as Victoria Island, in particular, is below sea level, much of Lagos could disappear beneath the waves.

Another reason for saving the rainforest is for its potential as a genetic storehouse for the development of the medicines and agricultural products of the future, as Chief Edu has mentioned in his foreword. Therefore, we destroy the rainforests at our peril, and if we continue to ignore this warning, who knows what might ultimately happen to Lagos?

Of course, it is not only vegetation which needs to be conserved; the wildlife population is important too. People often ask when conservation is mentioned, 'But how can we tell hunters to stop killing wild animals when their families do not have enough to eat?' The answer is to explain to them that wildlife reserves like Yankari are being established in order to protect the various species of birds and animals from extinction and to provide a healthy breeding stock for the future. From these reserves, wild animals will spread out into the surrounding areas where they can be hunted. However, unless these reserves are maintained and the animals outside the restricted areas are harvested in a sustainable way, eventually there will be no bush meat for the people at all. The aim of nature conservation, therefore, is to preserve the WHOLE environment, not only for birds and animals but for human beings as well, as our survival is dependent upon theirs.

Unfortunately, the pressures on protected areas will grow remorselessly unless the number of human beings is limited. Scientists believe that the population explosion is one of the most fundamental of all problems and the cause of most of the world's ills. Five billion people live on this earth and at least half a billion are hungry. The world population threatens to double every 40 years and the population of the developing world every 25 years, so an important step in preserving the earth's resources is to understand the need to have smaller families. We can think of it in terms of sharing out a cake. If there are 20 people at the party, everyone will get a very small slice of cake, but if there are only ten, each person will receive a sufficiently large slice to satisfy their hunger. Or, if we think of a forest as a savings account, we should only take out the annual growth (the interest) and leave the forest (the capital) intact.

Pollution is another major threat to the environment, whether from industrial gases emitted into the atmosphere by factories, the fumes from motor cars or harmful chemicals used in agriculture. If pollution is not seriously controlled, the future for all of us is bleak. Birds, because of the high rate of their metabolism and their furious pace of living, often reflect changes in the countryside before other living things do, so they serve as a sort of environmental litmus paper to test the health of our surroundings, like the Peregrines we discussed in the introduction. Birdwatchers, therefore, can become the 'Watchdogs of the Environment' as they notice decreases or changes in the bird population of an area, and try to discover the reason why this is happening. It does not usually take long to find out the causes. If steps are taken to put things right, the birds will soon be back.

The Plight of the White Stork

In the chapter on migration we looked in detail at the life history of the White Stork which is under threat at both ends of its migratory route. Now let us consider conservation in more particular terms by looking at the threats to this beautiful bird – a bird which has featured so prominently in the folklore of both Africa and Europe for centuries. The threat in Africa is from both habitat destruction and also human predation. As we have seen, the main wintering grounds for the White Stork population from Western Europe is West Africa and in Nigeria storks are mainly concentrated in the Hadejia-Nguru Wetlands in the north. The dangers of desertification to the area from overgrazing by domestic animals, and irrigation schemes diverting the water from the wetlands, have already been emphasised. The storks would have nowhere to go if this should happen as the habitat further south is forest and therefore unsuitable for them. The other danger is from men who trap the birds to be sold in

WHITE STORKS IN 'HOSPITAL' NGURU

the markets either for food or as pets. Storks are now protected birds and it is illegal to trap them at all, but it still continues. Think of the suffering such a bird experiences by being confined in a cramped cage in a crowded market, far from the waterside habitat where it normally lives? These birds, like Grey Parrots, are threatened species and once they are caged they will no longer breed, so that is the end of the line as far as these birds are concerned. These storks were photographed in the 'hospital' outside the Headquarters of the Hadejia Wetlands Project at Nguru, where their injuries were being tended. After recovery, they are released back into the wild.

If a White Stork has survived the dry season in Nigeria and the hazardous journey back to Europe across deserts, mountains and the Mediterranean Sea, then there are still further threats to its livelihood. In Europe many of the meadows around the villages where the storks nest, have been brought under more intensive cultivation and the marshes drained. The frogs and voles which are the storks' main food supply, can no longer survive, thus endangering the storks. Pylons and powerlines are also a major hazard, particularly for the young storks. These birds are inexperienced flyers and often crash into them with fatal results. Fortunately, some effort is now being made to put these powerlines underground, near villages where storks still nest. A captive breeding programme is also being carried out in The Netherlands, but the plight of these birds is an international problem as storks are inter-continental travellers. It would be sad indeed if these beautiful birds, celebrated in many an African fable, should be doomed through man's own destructive nature.

Sir David Attenborough and Ian Prestt recently wrote the following stark warning about the plight of birds in the world, in the foreword to their book Save The Birds: Literally hundreds of species are in serious danger of extinction. Each one is unique; the product of millions of years of evolution. But today, as many as one in ten of the world's birds could be under sentence of death. We are their executioners, sometimes with gun and trap, but mostly by our destruction of their habitats and degradation of the environment. We possess the power and the knowledge to halt the accelerating rate of extinctions. We must do so. We cannot bring back what is already gone; that is a loss that will impoverish the lives of our children and all future generations.

The late Sir Peter Scott, who was the Honorary Chairman of the World Wildlife Fund also wrote a very thought provoking statement in his foreword to The Birds of Singapore:
It has been said that a mark of civilisation is the importance which its people give to wild creatures. Development which shows no regard for them cannot be considered civilised development. Our planet is a living world and we are simply a small, but disproportionately destructive, part of it. Unless man can learn to live in harmony with his environment, the destruction of his natural heritage will demean his material achievements.

What is Being Done to Help Conservation in Nigeria?
The Nigerian Conservation Foundation (NCF) was founded in 1982 to promote nature conservation in Nigeria. It is a charitable trust whose activities include conservation education, support for wildlife research, the protection of endangered species and habitats, and lobbying the government for legislation to promote conservation. Its headquarters are at 5, Mosley Road, Ikoyi, Lagos, and in 1990 the Lekki Conservation Centre, a few kilometres outside Lagos on the Epe Road, was opened to provide a centre for conservation education for schools.

The NCF was formally linked to the World Wide fund for Nature (WWF) in February 1989, through an agreement signed during the visit of HRH Prince Philip, the Duke of Edinburgh, President of WWF International. Through this agreement, the NCF has been able to benefit from the WWF's worldwide reputation, as well as from its expertise in fund raising and the management of conservation projects.

Current NCF projects include:

1. RAINFOREST CONSERVATION PROJECTS
(a) The Okomu Wildlife Sanctuary (Edo State).
This was created in 1985 chiefly to protect the White-throated Monkey which is only found in Nigeria. However, the sanctuary also conserves an important area of the forest of south-west Nigeria. It is home to the forest Elephant, Buffalo, Sitatunga and the Red River Hog, as well as a huge variety of forest birds, including Great Blue Plantain-eaters, Grey Parrots and all the species of hornbills to be found in the high forests of West Africa. There are plans for an educational resource centre and an agro-forestry training centre to teach farmers improved farming methods which will then be passed on to their own communities.

(b) Cross River National Park
The large Oban section of this National Park contains the last remaining example of untouched primary rainforest in Nigeria. Its unique wildlife includes the Drill Monkey, Golden Potto, Red Colobus, Bate's Pygmy Antelope, Ogilby's Duiker and two rare birds, the Bare-headed Rock-fowl and the Olive Ibis. NCF and WWF have drawn up a plan to protect this area and begun a state-wide conservation education project together with the Institute of Education at the University of Calabar.

The northern Okwango section of the national park has a small population of Lowland Gorillas as well as interesting montane plants and bird species. The forest Elephant still survives here in good numbers too.

(c) Kagoro/Nindam Bird Sanctuary (Kaduna State)
This is an interesting lowland rainforest area on the southern escarpment of the Jos Plateau. A joint NCF/ICBP (International Council for Bird Preservation) team has studied the birds of the area and has made recommendations for their protection.

2. HADEJIA-NGURU WETLANDS CONSERVATION PROJECT

These wetlands, which span Jigawa, Yobe and Bauchi States, form an important wintering ground for Palearctic migrants, but also contain large numbers of resident waterfowl. For the local people too, they are vitally important for the fishing, dry season farming and grazing. A plan to manage the area is being developed by the Royal Society for the Protection of Birds (RSPB) and the World Conservation Union under a contract with the Federal Government and ICBP. The plan aims to make the best use of the whole wetlands system for both fishing and farming but at the same time maintaining the water-levels which are so important for the bird populations.

3. SUPPORT FOR EXISTING GAME RESERVES

The NCF gives both technical assistance and support for anti-poaching measures to existing game reserves. Together with WWF, management plans have been developed for Yankari Game Reserve, (Bauchi State), and the Gashaka-Gumti Reserve in Taraba State.

4. SPONSORING SCIENTIFIC EXPEDITIONS

The NCF, together with other conservation organisations, has sponsored expeditions to study endangered animals and birds including the Manatee, the Lowland Gorilla, the Bare-headed Rock-fowl and Sclater's Guenon. This Guenon is an endemic monkey only found in an extremely restricted area in Eastern Nigeria and probably one of the rarest monkeys in the world.

5. INITIATING A FUEL-EFFICIENT STOVE PROJECT

The aim of this project is to reduce the amount of firewood used in traditional ways of cooking by introducing a more fuel-efficient stove. It will prevent the sparse trees being cut down so rapidly and therefore help to control desertification, especially in the arid North of the country.

6. ENVIRONMENTAL EDUCATION

A pilot scheme to introduce Conservation Clubs in selected schools in Lagos, Edo and

Cross River States, has proved very successful and will soon be extended to other parts of the country. Environmental Education Units for the training of teachers and teacher-trainers have been set up at the University of Calabar, and the College of Education at Ekiadalor near Benin.

The overall aim of the NCF in launching these programmes is firstly, to promote the conservation of biological diversity, (the preservation of as many species of plants and animals as possible) through their support for existing game reserves and national parks throughout the country. Secondly, to encourage the sustainable use of these plants and animals outside reserves. This 'sustainable use' programme aims to encourage the non-destructive use of resources, such as tourism, controlled hunting, and sustainable logging, by managing the land so that people benefit from it rather than destroying it. Therefore, it can be seen that the NCF is dedicated to nature conservation in all its aspects although it has not yet been able to deal with the problems of either pollution or over-population.

Chapter Eleven

BIRDS IN AFRICAN FOLKLORE

Many African folktales used wild birds and animals as their central characters and wove spell-binding stories around these creatures. Sometimes the fables had a moral to them, but often these tales tried to explain the behaviour of birds and animals, demonstrating how previous generations in Africa lived much closer to nature and what excellent observers of natural history they were. One such tale is about the bird we now call the Senegal Coucal.

WHY THE COUCAL IS SUCH A FEEBLE BIRD, AND CAN ONLY FLY FOR SHORT DISTANCES

One day the birds were bragging about how strong they were. Even Sunbird, the smallest of them all, started to boast of his strength, and when Coucal heard him, he laughed and jeered at Sunbird; but Sunbird immediately challenged Coucal to a trial of strength. So they agreed that, for a wager, each one should build himself a house, and should go inside, and seal all the doors and windows. They were to see who could stay the longest inside his house without either food or drink.

Now Sunbird was very cunning, and although he left no doors or windows in his house unsealed, he did leave a tiny entrance underneath it.

The two birds then commenced their trial of strength. Towards evening, Sunbird called out to Coucal, 'Hullo! Coucal, are you there?' Coucal answered, 'I am all right, how are you?' 'Feeling strong,' said Sunbird. Now during the night, Sunbird went out of his house by the little entrance underneath, and went in search of food. Before it was light he was back again inside his house. Next morning , Sunbird called across to Coucal, 'How are you getting on, Coucal?' 'I am all right. How are you?' Coucal asked. 'Very strong,' said Sunbird. That night, Sunbird again went out in search of food. And so this went on for two or three days.

Every day, Sunbird called out cheerfully to Coucal, but Coucal's voice got weaker and weaker, until on the seventh day, there was no answer at all from Coucal. Sunbird then came out of his house and went to Coucal's, where he found Coucal prostrated, and hardly strong enough to whisper. Coucal had to admit that Sunbird had won the wager. But Coucal had become so weak, that he was never able to recover his strength in full again.

And that is why, even to this day, he is so feeble and is only able to fly short distances at a time.

(Reproduced by kind permission of the Editor of 'The Nigerian Field', the magazine of the Nigerian Field Society, Vol. VII No. 4, October 1938.)

Next time you see a Senegal Coucal, watch it flying, and you will see how accurately its flight has been described!

Some stories have been made into collections of folktales, and one such book is 'Hare and Hornbill' by Okot p'Bitek in the African Writers Series. The following two stories have been adapted from this book. The first one attempts to explain why owls are nocturnal and the second, why the hyena is so ugly.

WHY THE OWL DOES NOT FLY BY DAY

All the birds had gathered together to choose their chief, but there were many contenders vying for the title. Dove believed she should be the winner because of her beautiful cooing voice, but both Hawk and Eagle were arguing loudly that they should be chosen because of their strength. Owl too, was a powerful contestant, as some birds believed that a chief should be wise as well as strong. But in the end, as no one could agree, it was decided to hold a contest. The bird who could fly the furthest would become their chief.

At the sound of a drum, the birds took off with a flurry of excited wings, but in the confusion the crafty Swallow concealed himself on Eagle's back. Eagle soared high into the sky but when he finally tired and prepared to return to earth, Swallow flew off and soared higher still, so declaring himself the winner. However, when they discovered that Swallow had tricked them, the other birds were so angry that they threatened to kill him, and immediately began to chase him. In desperation, Swallow managed to escape by flying off in a zig-zag manner, then swooped into a hole in a termite mound to hide. Owl was tasked with guarding the hole carefully to see that Swallow did not escape, but he became so weary of keeping watch that he fell fast asleep, allowing the prisoner to fly off to freedom. When this was discovered, the birds were so angry with Owl that they threatened to roast him alive, and he only escaped by flying off into the thickest part of the forest to hide. That, the fable says, is why he is still frightened to come out by day, in case his enemies are, even now, waiting to catch him and roast him alive.

In this story, even the swift zig-zagging flight of the swallow has been carefully observed. A third fable tries to explain the curious skulking behaviour of the hyena, but a bird, Guinea Fowl, is the central character in this age-old story of reward and punishment.

GUINEA FOWL, LEOPARD AND HYENA

Once upon a time Leopard and Hyena both had the same dull brown-coloured fur. One day when Leopard was walking along the riverbank, he came across Guinea Fowl. The bird's attractive spotted plumage was much admired by Leopard so Guinea Fowl promised him that he would make his body as beautiful as his own if, in return, Leopard would provide a sumptuous feast for himself and his family. He told Leopard to kill a buck and bury it to allow the maggots to multiply, and then to call for him in four days time. After four days when the feast was ready, Leopard did as he was asked and called Guinea Fowl to the buck. When he and his friends had feasted themselves and could eat no more, Guinea Fowl tattooed his benefactor's skin with the beautiful spotted pattern that leopards wear to this day.

But when Hyena saw the beauty of Leopard's skin, he became very jealous and begged Guinea Fowl to tattoo patterns all over his body too. As before Guinea Fowl asked Hyena to provide a feast for himself and his family, promising in return to decorate his coat with beautiful spots like Leopard's. He told Hyena to kill an antelope, and bury it for four days until the maggots had multiplied and then call him to the feast when it was ready. However, the wicked Hyena cheated him by eating the flesh of the antelope himself, and burying only the horns and the bones, so after four days there were hardly any maggots for Guinea Fowl and his family to eat. The wily Guinea Fowl said nothing and set to work to tattoo Hyena's body, but when the work was finished and Hyena stood up, all the other animals began to roar with laughter because he looked so horribly ugly. This is why, the fable tells us, hyenas walk so stealthily to this day - because they are desperately ashamed of their ugly spotted skin!

Like all good fables, this one has an important moral lesson; that cheating never pays! Although, of course, this story is just make-believe, it is very descriptive of the furtive behaviour and ugly appearance of the hyena. However, today we know that hyena's are not the 'nasty' scavengers we once thought, but like lions, they often kill their own prey and have a very close-knit family life. But then, that is another story!

GLOSSARY

AQUATIC: living in, or near, water.

AVIFAUNA: a collective noun for birds.

BEAK: the mouthparts of a bird, also called a bill.

BILL: another name for a bird's beak.

BIRDS OF PREY: birds that kill and eat other animals, e.g. eagles, buzzards, falcons, etc.

CARRION: flesh of dead animals

CERE: a featherless patch of skin at the base of the beak, often yellow in colour.

CLUTCH: the total number of eggs which are laid at one time.

CREST: a tuft of feathers on the front or rear of the head.

CROP: a pouch-like part of a bird's gullet, used to store food.

CRYPTIC: plumage coloration which camouflages a bird.

DESERTIFICATION: the process by which dry lands turn to desert.

DIURNAL: active by day.

ECOLOGY: the study of the relationship between living things.

ECOSYSTEM: the way living things interact within their habitat.

EYE-STRIPE: a line of colour running through the eye.

FACIAL DISCS: flattened discs of feathers around a bird's eyes, especially owls, thought to act as sound receptors.

FLEDGLING: a young bird.

FOOD CHAIN: a network of living things which depend upon each other for food.

GAPE: the part of the beak that opens.

GIZZARD: the strong muscular part of a bird's stomach that often contains grit to help grind up food. In birds it can do the job of teeth.

GLIDING: flying by riding the air currents without flapping, while the wings are held outstretched.

HABITAT: the natural home of a plant or animal.

IITA: The International Institute for Tropical Agriculture

IMMATURE: a young animal or bird before reaching adulthood.

INCUBATE: to keep eggs warm in order for the embryo to develop.

INSECTIVOROUS: feeding on insects.

MANDIBLE: upper and lower parts of a bird's beak.

MIGRATION: regularly travelling long distances between two particular places, usually seasonally.

MOBBING: the attacking of a larger bird by a smaller bird or birds, in an attempt to chase it away.

MOULT: The normal shedding and replacing of feathers, usually at definite times of the year.

NICTITATING MEMBRANE: a third, semi-transparent eyelid to protect the eye.

NIDICOLOUS: young birds which are naked and helpless when hatched.

NIDIFUGOUS: young birds which are covered with down when hatched and able to run from the nest as soon as the down is dry.

NOCTURNAL: active by night.

NUPTIAL PLUMAGE: the pattern of feathers adopted during the breeding season.

OIL GLAND: a special gland at the base of the tail which produces oil for preening.

ORNITHOLOGY: the study of birds.

ORNITHOLOGIST: a person who studies birds.

PALEARCTIC: the arctic and temperate regions of the world.

PELLET: a regurgitated ball of indigestible pieces of food.

PLUMAGE: the body covering of feathers.

POLLUTION: when substances reach harmful levels in the environment.

PREDATOR: an animal that hunts and kills other animals.

PREEN: to clean and arrange feathers with the beak.

PREY: animals that are hunted and killed by other animals.

PRIMARIES: large wing feathers, or flight feathers

RAPTOR: diurnal bird of prey

REGURGITATE: to bring back food from the crop or stomach into the mouth.

ROOST: bird's perching or resting place.

SECONDARIES: feathers growing from the second joint of a bird's wing.

SHIELD: a hard horny plate from the base of the bill covering the forehead.

SPECIES: biological group of birds, animals, or plants with the same characteristics.

SUSTAINABLE MANAGEMENT: a way of managing the land so that we benefit from it without destroying it.

TALONS: large claws.

TERRITORY: an area in which a bird or animal lives and/or breeds.

THERMAL: a rising current of warm air.

WADERS: long-legged birds which wade in the water to feed.

WING-BAR: bands of different coloured feathers on the wings, often only seen in flight.

REFERENCES

Save The Birds Anthony W. Diamond, Rudolf L. Schreiber, David Attenborough,Ian Prestt. *Pro Natur/ICBP*

The Birds of Africa,Vols I, II and III Leslie H. Brown, Emil K. Urban, Kenneth Newman, Stuart Keith, C. Hilary Fry. *Academic Press*

The Birds of Tropical West Africa, Vols 1-8 David Bannerman. *Crown Agents*

The Birds of West and Equatorial Africa, Vols 1 and 2 David Bannerman. *Oliver and Boyd*

Field Guide to the Birds of West Africa W. Serle, G.J. Morel, W. Hartwig. *Collins*

The Birds of Nigeria John Elgood. *B.O.U. Checklist*

Birds of Africa John Karmali. *Collins*

Birds of the West African Town and Garden John Elgood. *Longman*

Secrets of Bird Life Ron Freethy. *Blandford*

The Trials of Life David Attenborough. *Collins/BBC*

World of Birds James Fisher, Roger Tory Peterson. *Crescent*

A First Book of Birds Peter Holden, J.R.T. Sharrock. *MacMillan*

How to begin the Study of Birds R. Freethy. *Richmond Publishing Company (with BNA)*

Birds of Prey Jill Bailey. *Young Naturalist Series*

Hare and Hornbill Okot p'Bitek. *African Writer's Series*

The Field Journal of the Nigerian Field Society, October, 1938

RSPB 'BIRDS' magazine Spring and Winter 1990

The Year of the Stork RSPB Video

INDEX OF BIRDS